ABOUT THE AUTHOR

Jonathan Goforth, ABR, SFR started his real estate career in 1998. After struggling his first two years as a realtor, his business started taking off with great success. Jonathan is a realtor with Reece and Nichols Real Estate, Kansas City's largest Real Estate Company, a partner with HomeServices of America, Inc., a Berkshire Hathaway affiliate. He is licensed in both Missouri and Kansas.

In 2008 Jonathan became the #1 Top Selling Agent in his office based on total volume and based on number of transactions. Jonathan has also listed more homes than any other agent in 2006, 2008, 2009 and 2010 in that same office. Kansas City Magazine ranks Jonathan as a top-level "Five Star Agent" for the past seven years. In April of 2009, Jonathan was selected to speak on the "All-Star Panel" of highest selling realtors.

The 25 Successful Tips outlined in this book helped Jonathan become a Top Selling Agent making him an overwhelming success in this tough housing market. Jonathan, his wife and three small children live in a suburb of Kansas City. They are active members at First Baptist Church in Raytown, Missouri, where Jonathan is a deacon. He has served on a variety of committees at that church and also in the community. Jonathan is a graduate of Missouri State University with a degree in Business & Marketing.

HOW TO SELL HOMES IN A TOUGH MARKET

25 Successful Tips Every Realtor Should Know

Hilarious Laugh-Out-Loud Examples to Help You Sell More Houses!

Jonathan F. Goforth

Kathy McCarty,
You are Tough enough!
Go forth and Sell!!

Jonathan Goforth

authorHOUSE®

AuthorHouse™
1663 Liberty Drive
Bloomington, IN 47403
www.authorhouse.com
Phone: 1-800-839-8640

First published by AuthorHouse 9/28/2011

ISBN: 978-1-4634-3392-5 (sc)
ISBN: 978-1-4634-3391-8 (hc)
ISBN: 978-1-4634-3390-1 (e)

Library of Congress Control Number: 2011912131

Printed in the United States of America

Jonathan Goforth's headshots were taken by Nazarethman Photography- Franklin Lugenbeel. www.NazarethmanPhotography.com

Any people depicted in stock imagery provided by Thinkstock are models, and such images are being used for illustrative purposes only. Certain stock imagery © Thinkstock.

This book is printed on acid-free paper.

ACKNOWLEDGMENTS

I am grateful to my clients for making me a successful real estate agent, and for providing the hilarious events in this book. To each client who has trusted me in serving them to buy and sell their most valuable possession, their Home, I humbly say Thank You!

My wife, Carrie, is fantastic at supporting my schedule and encouraging me to work. She has enjoyed laughing with me over the past few years as I'd tell her about the funniest things that happened each day. She encouraged me to begin writing the funny stories so I could always remember them. Who would have thought it would become the foundation for a book.

Along the way my Aunt Sondra suggested I write a book about real estate, and so the process began.

Our three children, Lydia (4 years old), Luke (2 ½ years old), and Caleb (1 year old), keep me motivated to work hard so I can provide for my family. Without the ongoing drama they create, our lives would be much less chaotic and fun. A few of the comical situations they have provided found their way into this book. They inspire me to strive for success.

Peggy Epstein, Cathy McClellan, Kathy Simmons, Joanna Goforth, Larry Jones and Sarah Barrows had significance on this book coming to completion. They not only brought forth editing skills, but motivated me to continue writing until the book was finished. My heartfelt appreciation goes to each of them for their hours of time and their encouragement.

My real estate brokers, Harvey and Dianna Kinnard are exceptional leaders in how they manage their office. They are the best brokers I have ever been privileged to work with! Their support of each agent in the office provides an environment that breeds success and creates an environment where I can flourish. Without Dianna's unfailing support and contagious enthusiasm, this book would never have been published.

I am grateful to God for His blessings on my career and family. God must truly have a wonderful sense of humor to allow so many hilarious situations to take place in my life on a regular basis. Having a belief in God and a relationship with Jesus Christ gives purpose to my life.

And most importantly, I thank YOU the reader, for taking time to read this book. Many months have gone into the writing and development in the hopes you will learn how to sell more homes in this tough housing market. I hope you will have a fantastic experience relating to the comical situations and that, with the help of this book, you will sell even more houses with great success.

Thank you!

Jonathan F. Goforth, ABR, SFR

TABLE OF CONTENTS

INTRODUCTION:

I was beginning my third year as a realtor, and I had new buyers who were under a deadline to pick a home before losing their apartment. We looked at nine homes and they narrowed it down to their top two choices. They weren't going to be available the next weekend, so we decided to look at their final two choices on Thursday, early in the morning before they went to work. I knew we might be pushing the homeowners out earlier than they would normally leave for work, so I called three days in advance to set up these two showings for 7am making sure I had confirmation.

Thursday morning arrived and I met the buyers at the first house, then we headed to the other one. I rang the doorbell a couple of times, opened the door and I ran upstairs to start turning on lights. As I was rushing along the upstairs hallway, the homeowner flung open the bathroom door about 6 feet in front of me completely naked! When she saw me she began screaming at the top of her lungs!

Have you ever been screamed at? I, instinctively, yelled even louder from the shock. I scared this woman so bad, she started flailing her arms about while frantically screaming and pleading, "Just take anything, but don't hurt me! *Please* don't hurt me!" It must have been her intent to leave the bathroom and head to her bedroom to get dressed, and a stranger in her hallway was the last thing she expected. Perhaps she was still in the shower as I rang the doorbell and didn't hear it, but nevertheless there we were.

This woman, probably in her late 50's, was so loud with her screaming that my buyers ran out the front door, and I almost wet myself from the shock. I'm amazed I didn't go tumbling backwards down the stairs! I tried to converse with her as I backed away trying to inform her that I was the realtor and we were all there to see her house again. She, still screaming as loud as possible, informed me she thought we were supposed to be there the next morning. I, now yelling back, let her know we were all supposed to be there right now, and she needed to put some clothes on. We immediately left the house, went back to my office, and the buyers wrote a contract on the other house.

How to Sell Homes in a Tough Market

Have you ever had a wonderful night of sleep when you dreamed you were rich? You woke up so happy and excited …and then reality hit and you realized "Uh oh, it was just a dream." I'm excited to announce you are in a career with absolutely no income limitation or cap whatsoever. You probably got into real estate because you've noticed certain realtors have made enormous amounts of money …and it appears they don't work very hard. Contrary to any previous job you might have had, being a successful realtor will offer you more advantages than you've ever dreamed of. This book is to encourage and motivate you to use 25 Successful Tips to take your real estate career to a whole new level. Perhaps you are a brand new agent with no idea what to do. Perhaps you've been in real estate for years, but now find yourself in a slump needing to jump start your sales.

Stand up and draw a line out in front of you with your foot. On *your* side of the line is your life right now. Every decision, big and small, that you've made since the day you were born has led you to exactly where you are right now. As you look over the line into the future where you have yet to step, you look toward all that you would like your life to become. All the dreams and visions in your heart lay waiting over the line. A Real Estate career is perhaps the most challenging and also most rewarding form of sales. Included in this book are 25 Successful Tips you should be doing. Most realtors don't do them consistently, and it's no surprise that most realtors are frustrated with their lack of sales.

These are the secrets that separate the Top Producing Realtors from everyone else. Rick Warren wrote in <u>The Purpose Driven Life</u>, "Nothing matters more than knowing God's purposes for your life, and nothing can compensate for not knowing them." If you believe that being a realtor should be your current vocation, and you aim to be a success at it, then this book will give you the tools and encouragement to take your real estate career to a whole new level.

It can be overwhelming thinking back to a life of decisions that have led you to the point that you've decided to read this book. I've never heard of anyone having their ultimate goal in life to become a realtor... it certainly wasn't on my list of "most sought after jobs" while in college. It wasn't until I started a new career in real estate that I realized how tough sales could be. Ironic that this would be my favorite job, yet it seems most real estate agents come from some other industry and just sort of end up here. Maybe they got laid off from their job, or they've had other sales jobs that didn't work out. Maybe they've been at home raising their kids and this career offered the flexibility to fit their schedule.

The current economy has drastically impacted our housing market. People are out of work, with many companies still laying off. Even many real estate agents are quitting who have failed to survive in this business. As more agents quit, the new agents signing up will be able to create a foundation that will position them for great success as the market rebounds in the upcoming months. This could possibly be the very best time in history for a new agent to enter the real estate industry.

My first two years in real estate were horrible. If you are struggling and wondering how much longer you can survive with no sales then I know exactly what you're going through. It took me a lot longer to become a successful realtor than I expected - but I have become a success. It was in 2008, ten years after I started, when I became the #1 Top Selling Agent in my office. What an achievement! We were already in a tough real estate market by 2008, and since that time the economy and real estate market have continued to worsen and it has become even more difficult to do any of our jobs like we used to.

Is anyone selling homes in this tough market? YES! My goal is to help you become a great success in real estate. Look at the line you've drawn in front of you. Everything you've ever dreamed of lies ahead. Do you want to achieve financial independence while you're young enough to enjoy it? Do you want a happier marriage? Do you want to enjoy spending more time with your kids? Do you want respect in the eyes of others for being a success? Perhaps you just want the satisfaction of knowing you helped a buyer enjoy homeownership for the first time. You can have all this, *if* you do what it takes to cross that line. This could possibly be the first time in your life where you actually have control of your future. If you have enough passion, commitment and a plan of action you can accomplish anything in life.

#1   How Strong Is Your Desire to Succeed?

EACH TIME I READ A new real estate book, I want the author's secrets. I want to know exactly what they did that created their success. What did they do to get their business off the ground? What gave them the momentum to keep it going? What sets that agent apart from most other agents out there? I want their most well-kept secrets on how to become a success.

Would you believe I'm actually going to give you my secrets? When I first started making an outline of what I had done to become successful, I was afraid of someone stealing my notes and using all my ideas. But then it occurred to me that most people can learn the secrets of what it takes to change whatever they want about themselves, but few actually do what it takes to become that changed person. It took me a while to become comfortable sharing my secrets from the fear everyone would surpass me in sales. I gave some suggestions to a new agent in my office a couple of years ago, but then I stated "Don't tell anyone else, we can't have everyone else being a success, now can we?" I was sort of joking, but I realized after that agent quit, he didn't put the hard work into his Real Estate career. He did nothing with the tips I gave him, he did nothing to create an action plan to advance his career, and he therefore did nothing in real estate.

The Tao of Warren Buffet is a book full of wise aphorisms. Aphorism #14 says "The chains of habit are too light to be felt until they are too heavy to be broken." How badly do

1

you want to step over the line and begin living the dream that many successful realtors enjoy every day? You will need to make some changes in your current work habits. In that same book, Warren Buffett's #69 aphorism states that "If you let yourself be undisciplined on the small things, you will probably be undisciplined on the large things as well."

Why is it important to study successful tips that have helped other people reach their dreams? "Understanding the cause of *failure* is important, but understanding the cause of *success* is far more powerful!" stated by Ed Oakley, co-author of <u>Enlightened Leadership: Getting to the Heart of Change</u>.

How strong is your personal desire to succeed as a realtor? You must understand your needs, just as you must understand your clients' needs. When you begin taking on sellers and buyers, everything is about them, but this book is about *you*. When you look at the new agents in your office, you see a variety of people all with different needs. A few agents will be single, some divorced or some never married. Their careers must become profitable quickly or they will have to find another income. Some agents might be married to spouses making lots of money, and these agents really don't have to make money to survive at all. Or perhaps an agent in your office has been a housewife for the past 10 years, but now that her kids are older she wants to get back in a flexible working environment.

Perhaps you've been in sales for a few years, but just got laid off and need a new job. With few companies hiring, you got into real estate as a last resort. You're in desperate need of money, and you have a few short months left before your savings run out. I, too, struggled for income, and it's for you this book is written. There will be many obstacles in the way, but I believe <u>we</u> are own biggest obstacle. To succeed, you must adopt the attitude of "I'm going to become a successful realtor, or I'm going to die trying." With that kind of hardcore work ethic, you will become a success. The successful tips in this book will work. They worked for me, and they've worked for countless other agents who have struggled. How bad do you *need* to succeed? When you take a listing, the price will be determined by the needs of your client. What are *their* motivating factors to reduce their price, or improve the condition of their home? How bad do *they* need to sell?

What are *your* motivating factors for doing the hard work it will take to succeed as a realtor? If you are married to a spouse with a high paying job and you simply got into real estate more as a hobby, then you might not have the same motivating factors as other realtors. If, however, you are the primary income provider for your family, then let's get you on the right path to making a lot of money as a top selling realtor.

YOUR BROKER NEEDS YOU TO BE A SUCCESS

Think of your broker as your cheerleader. Brokers are there only for one purpose: *Your* Success. They are there to cheer you on. They are *your* biggest fan. They need *you* to have a winning season. They can't survive without successful agents in their office. The more their agents sell, the more success for the broker. Think of your broker as your coach with the game plan. They have their finger on current trends and future forecasting. They have an offensive and defensive staff to make the team operate the best it can. If you've been sitting on the sidelines watching other agents play the game, then you need to be on the field. Your broker wants you on the field as much as you want to be there. Brokers are ranked by many categories, but it all comes down to how many houses that office sells. Successful agents selling a lot of houses make for a very happy and successful broker. You need to spend time in the office to get to know your broker better. Ask for advice. If your broker gives you a CD of some speaker they just heard, then listen to it while driving and give it back quickly to get more. If they have "new agent classes" in your office, then you need to attend. The better your relationship with your broker, the greater your chance of succeeding. We have new agents in my office on a regular basis. Some succeed quickly and some struggle, but on occasion we get new agents we never even see. They never come in the office, they never attend sales meetings, so they must have a full-time job elsewhere and probably have no time to do real estate. But if they aren't taking this real estate career thing seriously, how can they ever succeed at all? Make an effort to communicate with your broker regularly. Let them know what you are doing. Ask for their help on conducting open houses and marketing yourself. If you do have a job elsewhere to pay the bills, then communicate with your broker via phone and email until you can begin coming into the office. Find other successful agents in your office to listen to. Don't ever be embarrassed to ask for their time. Even if you have sold nothing for months, don't think your broker doesn't have time for you.

There are two ways to get started in Real Estate: either by joining a team of other agents or by starting as an individual agent. If you're on a team, then you believe and hope that your team leader is going to give you a huge head start by giving you buyers and sellers (listings). Hopefully that happens for you because that's the biggest advantage in joining a team. But if you want your own name recognition, a team won't be able to give it to you. If you want to control your own success and develop your own personal stable business you need to start as an individual agent and create a foundation to give *you* future referrals. Basically whose name do you want people to see on that for sale sign, *yours* or a team leader's name? Either way can make you money, it just depends on *your needs* and reasons for getting into real estate.

When I was in college getting my degree from Missouri State University, I majored in Business. Why? I'm not ashamed to tell you I wanted to make money. In fact I can say that looking back over my last few years, I've thoroughly enjoyed the times I made money, much more than the times I didn't.

Since college, most of my jobs have been in sales of some sort. No matter what products I was selling, the market always seemed oversaturated with salespeople. Have you noticed that? It's hard to break into a new market. With so much competition, I was always challenged to get my foot in the door wherever I went, and it was always hard work. Prospective businesses always seemed to be under existing leases or long-term service plans, and there was no way I could get them to change to my services until their contracts were over. There were always legitimate frustrations keeping me from being the success I wanted to be. Sound familiar? It became a tiresome numbers game, going through dozens of cold calls to find an occasional real prospect. But over time, some of those prospects became customers, and I became successful in the eyes of my boss. When I achieved and even exceeded my goals, they were then increased for the following year, making it harder to achieve again. I actually got penalized for being successful!

The reason I became a realtor? The former company where I worked was headed into financial trouble. I was working harder, but making less, and since the company was struggling financially, I decided to do something different with my life. When that company did go out of business, I decided I wanted to be self employed. I wanted a job where I couldn't get laid off, and I was also tired of working harder just to make my manager look good and having him take the credit.

So why real estate? It was the least expensive way to become self-employed and, to be honest, it seemed all the other realtors were getting rich and not working very hard. So I took my naive self to a "Realtor Career Night" where I learned I could make as much as I wanted. The income potential seemed endless, and I was hooked.

All of sudden, I was thrown into a sea overpopulated with real estate agents. Everywhere I looked other people were getting their real estate licenses too, and my rapid success didn't happen. Living on 100% commission and not selling much can quickly become the most negative and crushing experience to a person's self image.

There I was, a 29-year-old struggling, brand new realtor, and like many new agents, I sold nothing for months. The turnover of new agents coming into the business and quitting was astounding me! Why were so many agents failing at selling houses? I was quickly becoming one of them, but I consistently did a few things that eventually led me to sell houses – lots of houses.

In the book The Shark and the Goldfish by Jon Gordon, he writes "What fear and faith have in common is a future that hasn't happened yet. Fear believes in a negative future. Faith believes in a positive future. Interestingly enough, both believe in something that hasn't happened yet. ...Why not believe that great things are coming your way?"

You Have More Control Over Your Success Than You Realize

The greatest significance in being a realtor is how much control we have over our own success. If a struggling realtor knew what actions to take to create an environment where success could flourish, can you imagine the results? Be committed to some challenging tasks you might not have planned to take on. Some of them will be time consuming with no immediate reward. One thing is for sure, if you have a plan of action and stick to it you'll find yourself eventually selling more than many other realtors in your office. You'll become defined by the success you create. You'll be known throughout your area as a Top Selling Realtor and future clients will seek you out to list their homes.

A quick overview of my first two years in the business: At the age of 29 I got my real estate license. My first full year in real estate was so bad that I sold only one house, and it was a buyer under $85,000. I was discouraged and embarrassed. At the end of that year, it was suggested that perhaps I leave that real estate company because I was bringing down the average sales per agent, and go work for a different real estate company or maybe pursue a different career altogether. It was such a shocking wake up call to me that I asked to stay, promising I would try harder and would soon be selling houses. If I didn't succeed as a realtor then I would have to re-enter the corporate world of sales, and that was not my goal anymore.

Many weeks passed with me selling nothing again. It took months before my next sale. By the end of my 2nd year I had sold a few homes, but not enough to survive on. By the end of that year, I had invested so much money into mailings and other expenses that I was considering quitting just to stop the spending. My 3rd year improved much more compared to the first two years, and my 4th and 5th years were absolutely incredible as I sold numerous homes and my income climbed rapidly. It was so much fun making lots of money! The economy was thriving during those years and the real estate market was exploding with appreciation. Back then the turnover rate for realtors was still very high. Agents came and went, but I had found my career and I loved it! I had arrived, finally enjoying the income and benefits this career gives.

Perhaps you were a successful Realtor just a few years ago when the market was thriving, but lately you're just not selling as much. Following these successful tips will help you reclaim your market share. You need to develop an attitude that you'll be a success or die trying. So, how strong is your desire to succeed?

#2   Hello??? Are You Listening?

MY WIFE, CARRIE, COMPLAINS ABOUT this all the time to me. "You never listen!" But in reality I do hear her – most of the time. The problem is I'm not really engaged in the conversation, so I don't remember what she says sometimes. And just for the record, it's not all the time.

The most important thing to ensure success in selling is *listening* to our customers. No matter whether we sell cars, copy machines or houses, listening to our customers is the most important thing. Listening comes easily for me, but it's the *remembering* what was just said that I struggle with. Since each client has a specific need driving them to sell or buy a house, we must listen and find that need. We can then position ourselves as the solution.

I have this same "remembering" problem when I first meet people. I should listen for their names and I should remember them. I can spend all day preparing for an appointment. I put effort into how I look, how my breath smells, the cleanliness of my car... but for some reason a new client's name escapes me. We only get one opportunity to meet a client for the first time, and they always say their name. They give you a business card, but maybe they used a nickname when they shook your hand. Did you remember the nickname? Those little things will define your relationships as you get to know people better. There comes a point in a relationship when it's not acceptable to ask for their name – again.

Let's say you see someone at church. You only see them once a week usually, but you've been speaking in passing for months. You think you remember their name, but you're just not sure, so you never call them by name. How embarrassing when they always remember yours. How many times is it acceptable to ask, and re-ask for a person's name? It always makes me feel good when people use *my* name, so why then do I struggle to remember theirs? In Dale Carnegie's book, <u>How to Win Friends and Influence People</u>, he states, "Remember that a person's name is to that person the sweetest and most important sound."

Some people like me have a name that is commonly shortened. Most Jonathans probably go by John. Most Michaels probably go by Mike. Most people go by nicknames, but some people like me do not. If you want to irritate me, call me John and see how that goes for you. I never wanted to be called John growing up and I still don't. It amazes me how some people automatically shorten it thinking we'd be better buddies. It's important to listen to how people introduce themselves. If they use a nickname, then that's the name you call them. But if they keep it more formal, then you shouldn't shorten their name at your own discretion. Of the numerous "people skills" books I've read, they almost always stress the important of calling people by their names. There are even techniques to help memorize names quickly. There are all kinds of association techniques to help people like me remember names easier. I think the biggest problem is we forget to listen carefully when we hear their names the first time – and we don't realize we missed it until five minutes later. My wife had me list this tip near the beginning of the book, because it is still a constant struggle for me.

In this business we develop relationships with new people on a regular basis. Listening and remembering becomes the most valuable habit we can ever develop. When we use our clients' names on a regular basis, it gives us confidence in the relationship and makes them feel important. This all sounds great in a perfect world, but here's what often happens to me. I meet brand new clients to show them houses. We introduce ourselves and I take them out to see properties. I'm driving us around and along the way I realize - "Oops I'm not sure if I can remember their names." I start to panic thinking how I can get them to say their names again. I realize, ah yes, I'll have them write down their phone number and they should put their names next to it. That usually works, but sometimes they just put their phone number only – assuming I have remembered their names. So then I'll ask for their email address hoping their names are in it. It's shocking how many people's emails have nothing to do with their names.

After a few failed experiences, I now write down clients' names as soon as I hear them. I always have a file with me or papers on the houses I'm about to show and I write their names on the cover or on the papers I'm holding. Most of the time I already know their names from talking over the phone, but I always write their names at the top of my papers so I have it in front of me.

If you really want to score points and set yourself apart with your people skills, learn their kid's names too. Remember their pet's names. If you can't remember the name of their teenager who just went off to college, it's hard to ask how they're doing in a month. Let's say a grandparent is visiting your clients that week while you are at their house on an appointment. The rest of the family introduces you to the grandparent when you arrive. It would be respectful to remember that grandparent's name and use their name when you leave and say that you enjoyed meeting them also.

Over the course of taking buyers to look at homes, you'll get to know them better and better. The same is true of sellers when you list their home. I've had listings that took over a year to sell, and let me tell you, I felt like one of their family by the time we were finished! The better you are at developing relationships in this business the more successful you will become, and it all begins with paying attention to their names.

On every listing appointment I print the tax record on the house so I know the owner's names. On this particular listing appointment, it stated a husband and wife, so I was all set with their names. When I arrived, the husband let me in and introduced himself with, what I realized later, was his middle name. There was no middle name on the tax record I printed out, just a middle initial, so I made sure to remember what he wanted me to call him and I wrote it down. Then he introduced me to his wife. For some reason I didn't pay too much attention. All I knew is I had her name printed on the tax record. He used her name a couple more times as they showed me the house. I failed to remember though. The problem? They explained along the way that his first wife, the one listed on the tax record, had passed away and he had remarried. Oops. I hadn't paid attention to the new wife's name. Oh no! So as they told me all this information, I was trying to remember this new wife's name. He'd already said it maybe 5 times during conversation. Karen? Or Kathy? Or Carol? Or Carmen? I was hoping he would say it again, but he didn't. How embarrassing when I had to ask for her name at the end.

Do you attend Chamber of Commerce meetings? Everyone usually has a nametag. Let's say there are 50 people at the luncheon. I used to rarely even make an attempt to learn their names because there was no point when we were always labeled with big nametags. I learned a costly lesson at a gas station immediately after a chamber luncheon one time when a man from the chamber was pumping gas next to me. He sure remembered <u>my</u> name. He said he wanted to sell his house and told me to look him up in the chamber directory to get his phone number, then he got in his car and drove off. I had no idea who he was and I could not remember his name. There were hundreds of names and businesses in the Chamber directory. I had no idea where to start. By the next meeting, his house was listed by somebody else.

The better you are at developing relationships in this business the more successful you will become, and it all begins with listening.

#3 SURPRISE! PREPARE YOURSELF FOR A SHOCK!

HOW WE REACT TO SURPRISES in life is very important. Sometimes we need to stay calm and react as if nothing out of the ordinary is taking place. Sometimes we have to think on our feet and keep composure when unexpected things happen. Sometimes we need to defuse an awkward situation. Being able to adapt as needed will give successful agents an advantage in working with clients.

One time in our conference room I was sitting with Mr. & Mrs. Buyer, and we had just finished filling out the entire contract. Their two-year-old daughter seemed most content sitting on top of the table where we supplied her with crayons and her own contract to write on. It had been a good day of looking at houses, and their daughter was the best behaved little girl I'd ever seen – until she vomited all over the table. Unfortunately she soaked the contract and my expensive calculator. No problem. We simply filled out another contract quickly and life was right back on track. I never liked that calculator anyway.

On another occasion I had an appointment to list a house for a family I had never met before, so I put in extra effort to make a good first impression. They called me because we have a friend in common who gave them my phone number. This was a beautiful home, and I desperately wanted this listing. I made sure I looked good and smelled good – then I took a deep breath as I started walking up their driveway.

I was a little anxious because there was so much to remember.

I had a checklist of things I would need to bring: calculator, pen, for sale sign, tape measure, etc. It's always important to have information on their neighborhood printed out. What are other houses selling for close by? How long on the market? And how do those compare with this particular house? In this instance I had done all my homework and I was thoroughly prepared. I had even personally previewed two of the comparable houses for sale in the same neighborhood so I could appear more knowledgeable.

Sometimes, however, one can be only so prepared and something unexpected happens. In this case I had a 7:00pm appointment hoping to list this particular home. My sweet wife had cooked a new pasta dish for dinner that I ate quickly and headed to the appointment. I arrived at 6:55pm and everything was great. The homeowners both met me at the door and I remembered not only their names, but also their kid's and even their dog's name. I took notes as they showed me around and we sat at the dining room table and I got to know them a little better. Then I asked, "Did you want to go ahead and fill out the paperwork to list your house tonight?" They agreed! Yahoo! And they started filling out the Seller's Disclosure.

THIS IS EXACTLY HOW A PERFECT LISTING APPOINTMENT SHOULD GO

While sitting there at their dining room table, my stomach made an odd shifting noise – a loud high-pitched squall somewhere from the depths below. At this point I should mention that when I eat oily food, especially when combined with stress, I have stomach issues. I immediately broke into a severe sweat and I clenched, holding on as long as possible. Having heard that intestinal sound in the past, I dreaded what was to come. I closed my eyes for a moment pleading with God to help me through the appointment. The lovely homeowners were making good progress on filling out the disclosure, but then they paused with a question. I hurriedly answered it and then there was a great silence like in a library while they filled out more. That's when a much louder shifting sound came from the depth of my bowels. It was so awkward! I squeezed as tight as possible as I squirmed in the chair hoping the noise would cease. I'm sure they heard it the first time too, but this time the wife asked, "Are you alright?" I realized I was in need of a bathroom - preferably one at the other end of the house. So, embarrassed, I asked, "Do you think I could use your bathroom?" Mrs. Seller pointed right behind me about 3 feet - a bathroom door to the half bath off the entryway. I went in and saw a two-inch gap of light under the door. I flipped on the light and the exhaust fan. It was the quietest little exhaust fan I'd ever heard. I tried really hard to be quiet, barely relaxing. I begged and pleaded with God for no noises, but instead I exploded with the loudest sounds a person could make. It went on forever. After 15 minutes, I came back to the table with my tie and dress shirt loosened and my hair soaked with sweat. I was so embarrassed as I sat at the table, but we made it through the rest of the papers as fast as possible.

I learned that sometimes I can only be so prepared, and in spite of myself, I'll still end up making the sale. Funny they didn't shake my hand when I left, but one thing is for sure: When you are as prepared as possible, even an unnerving surprise shouldn't do you in. You might muddy up the waters a bit, but you'll still come out victorious.

On rare occasion, the sellers will be home for a showing creating awkward situations. I once had a Ms. Buyer with me and we were looking at duplexes. Some of the properties I had been showing her were vacant and some were rented, so I had to make sure I had showing confirmations in case renters needed to leave. On this beautiful spring day I was showing Ms. Buyer four properties. She would nicely comment each time we saw a property where she thought "good Christian folk" lived. Sometimes there would be Christian books on the nightstand, or religious information on their refrigerator, or maybe religious knickknacks sitting around on tables. She was always impressed when she could tell the homeowners or renters had a religious tone in the home. As she walked around looking at properties, she would hum praise songs and she really was a nice woman to drive around. After we saw a few properties, we went to a half-duplex that the MLS sheet said was currently rented. I assumed the renters would be gone, but after I rang the doorbell a college guy let us in, holding a beer. He knew we were coming and told us to look around. When we went in the living room there were two friends or roommates also drinking beer watching "Spring Break Gone Wild" on a big screen TV. Ms. Buyer looked at me with a raised eyebrow, and we went to look at the bedrooms. Everything was okay until we entered the hall bathroom and there she noticed a stack of Penthouse magazines on the back of the toilet. She whispered to me, "You know somebody needs to share Jesus with these young men." We went to the master bedroom, which actually showed well. The bed was made and dirty clothes hidden. But unfortunately two centerfolds were taped up behind the door. When she saw those, she went ballistic! She stormed right back to the living room, and with both hands raised high in the air she announced in a loud voice, "There's an evil spirit in this house and in the name of Jesus I'm gonna cast it out!"

She then stood behind the chair of the closest young man, laying her hands on his shoulders. While he lowered his beer she began speaking in tongues for the devil to leave his body. We all stared in amazement! It was something to behold! I didn't know what to do. I had *never* been taught how to deal with a situation like this in my real estate classes. As a Southern Baptist I was caught off guard with someone speaking in tongues, especially while showing rental properties. After maybe a minute of loud intense prayer she informed them, "Your mommas would be ashamed of you! Get those magazines out of this house and get yourselves to church!" And with that she turned to me and said

"Come on. We got houses to see!" And we were off to the next duplex.

Recently, I showed houses to a new couple I'd never met before. They work with one of my friends who always tries to refer clients to me. So we went looking at five homes. On the third house, we had been through the entire main floor and entered the master bedroom, me first with Mrs. Buyer right behind me. She wanted to see how big her closet would be. Mr. Buyer was right behind her. Entering the master bedroom, I stopped so abruptly that Mrs. Buyer literally ran into me, then Mr. Buyer ran into her. As I bent over to pick up all the papers I had dropped, Mrs. Buyer made a sort of shocked gasping sound. She saw the large naked man asleep on his bed (face down I should quickly mention). I'll give him credit that the sheet mostly covered his hairy rear end, but not quite enough to keep it a secret he was not wearing any underwear. He informed us that he was just taking a quick nap. He rose just slightly and covered himself up instructing us to pass through to the master bath. We quickly looked around and left. Sometimes we have to think on our feet when the unexpected happens.

As a realtor, you will find yourself in the midst of bizarre situations that demand we think on our feet and keep our composure. We never know what can turn off a buyer from a home that might actually be the perfect fit for them. Some clients can be personally offended by something that has nothing to do with the actual property. We have to remind our clients to stay focused on their needs and overlook distractions, especially when a property might not show its best side.

#4 SPREAD THE GOOD NEWS!

L ET THE WORLD KNOW, YOU are a Real Estate Agent! Have you absorbed this identity into your very being? It's who you are now. So, how many people know you sell houses? Are you keeping it a secret? The bottom line is: The more people who know you sell houses, the more houses you will sell. The biggest question you'll always be asking yourself is, "Where is my next sale coming from?" You'll need buyers and you'll need sellers (Listings). That's all you need, and it's just that simple. So, how do you get sellers and buyers?

THE BOTTOM LINE IS "THE MORE PEOPLE WHO KNOW YOU SELL HOUSES, THE MORE HOUSES YOU WILL SELL."

Everything in this book supports that bottom line. As I began writing this book, I made the assumption that the people reading it would mostly be new agents. As word spread in my office that I was staying up many late nights writing a book, I was surprised how many experienced agents wanted to read it too. It would appear they also wanted secrets on how to sell in a tough market.

When the market was thriving, agents were selling so many homes that it was hard to keep up. When you're that busy, who has time to prospect? But with the housing market turning downward for many agents, they now need to do something to give their business a boost. If you want to know how much you'll be selling over the next three months, look in your pipeline. Your pipeline is your future business. Sometimes you'll go on a listing appointment, but before you have them sign papers and put the sign in the yard, they need to do some improvements. Do they need to repaint some rooms, or re-carpet? Maybe a new roof is coming, or they need to seriously de-clutter the entire main floor. So you leave without listing the home, but you know it's in your pipeline as future business. Perhaps you go on various listing appointments during the winter, or during your slowest season, and many of these sellers simply want to see what you think their house will sell for. They're getting ready to list their house and just want information in advance to prepare before the busy season starts. You'll get lots of these that feed into your pipeline.

Your Pipeline Should Always Have Future Business Lined Up in It

Perhaps you're also getting some buyers in the very near future - as soon as their daughter gets married, or as soon as school gets out they'll start looking at houses. Maybe it's a family friend and as soon the husband retires in a couple of years they are moving out of state and will need to sell their home. Your pipeline gives you confidence and security of good things to come. But if your pipeline ever dries up, you are in very big trouble.

For this reason, you must always be prospecting. After years of research asking clients, "How did you select your realtor?" the #1 category is always from their circle of influence. They picked their agent because they were a friend, or in the family, or got referred to them from a friend, or by a coworker, or fellow church member, or knew them from the gym, or from a past job. All these things make up your circle of influence (COI). Let's call it a "Community of Influence". I repeat, the more people who know you sell houses, the more houses you will sell. The most exciting news is your COI list is FREE! You're not buying leads, or running newspaper ads, or trying to get people from an open house, or cold calling from the phone book. All these other avenues can be good to get clients too, but nothing is as great as your community of influence. This says to me, whoever has the biggest COI wins! There are many ways to spread the good news to these people ….but first you need an organized name list.

IN FACT YOU *MUST* HAVE A NAME LIST

Without an organized and up-to-date name list, your road from point A to point B will be long and bumpy and you'll likely quit from frustration. You'll simply take too long, probably run out of money and be forced to find another job to pay the bills. Don't be like many other agents who get into Real Estate and never put together an organized name list. You need names, addresses, phone numbers and email addresses. Take that information and create a spread sheet in your computer, or use some way to organize your database of names. You should have two lists: List A and List B. You need a way to print labels and easily sort the list by last name, or by zip code or city. This name list will eventually become the most important thing you own. It will be your primary way of making future income for years to come. Use the pages in the back of the book to write down names as they cross your mind to increase your COI list.

Let's say a brand new bank has just appeared in your city. It's located on a fairly busy intersection that you've been passing every day. The sign just went up on it yesterday advertising that it's a new bank. Let's take the manager of the bank as our case study for a moment. He is going to run this new bank in your city, and your city probably has no shortage of banks already. In my city it seems like banks are on every other corner. Some of the larger banks have numerous locations even in the same part of the metro. It's crazy! So, how do they all stay in business? How do they all pay their rent, utilities, and staff in each location? The manager of this brand new bank is probably wondering what to do. First, he needs to spread the good news that his bank is open for business, just like you as a new realtor. He is fortunate to have a large sign on the building, but if that's his only announcement it won't be enough to get people in the door. The problem is everybody who already has money is already using a different bank. There will have to be some compelling reason for people to change who they are currently using. This new bank needs people to walk inside and open new checking accounts, new savings accounts, open CD's, take out a house loan or car loan with them. How does this bank accomplish that when the market is already saturated with other banks? There is a very big difference between making people aware the bank exists and actually soliciting them to use them for business. Just like you, spreading the good news you're a realtor isn't enough. You need to prospect, you need to be contacting new people, and you need to be soliciting everybody you come in contact with to use you as their realtor when the time comes. This will generate new leads for you.

IT ALL STARTS WITH BUILDING RELATIONSHIPS WITH PEOPLE

Rich Casto, one of the nation's top Real Estate Trainer/Coaches, has trained over 35,000 agents and brokers. He says "If you touch a prospect 6 times, then 85% of them don't have a choice but to remember you." You need to create an action plan of how you will consistently remind people you are a realtor while building relationships with them.

The new bank needs an action plan to succeed, and so do you. Make a list of everyone you have a relationship with and create an Action Plan to remind them over and over and over that you sell houses. The better you are at *name branding* yourself, the more successful you will become. Did you realize you would be prospecting when you signed up to be a realtor? Most new agents expected this business to be quite easy and the minute they walked in their broker's office they would get a list of new clients. They expected their broker to say, "Here, just call these people and go list their houses. They're all expecting your call." Oh, how I wish it was that easy!

Would you believe when I was new, I thought I could take board duty in the office and get so many phone calls of new people wanting to sell that I'd get rich? Can you believe any agent would have expectations like that? The biggest shock and disappointment for new agents is realizing prospecting is very hard work. It's time consuming, possibly expensive and will bring on a lot of rejection. Everything in this book is dependent on good prospecting, and it all starts with building relationships with people. Without clients there is no reason to read the real estate contract. It makes no difference if you plan on remembering your client's kids names if you have no appointments to go meet them. Skills such as conducting open houses, learning how to negotiate, keeping up with what's for sale, and knowing the daily interest rates come only after prospecting. If you don't build relationships with people, you will die a quick death in this business.

Having current clients and future clients, those in your pipeline, are like air to your body. Without continuous air, you suffocate. With proper air, your body functions as it should. Your heart beats, and your arms and legs move you around successfully. If you try running you require even more air. You breathe deeper because it's needed to maintain a faster speed for your body to thrive. You've created momentum and it takes a lot more air to maintain. Prospecting is the life-blood of your real estate business.

You Must Have New Clients

This bank also needs new clients. It needs air to breathe and survive. So, how is this bank going to prospect? How is it going to get new customers? If this bank has a new name which no one has heard of it's going to be tough, but definitely not impossible. If this bank puts together a good action plan with some effective marketing, it will succeed. It will possibly even thrive in a saturated banking environment. The one advantage you have over this bank is you have a community of influence (COI). If you want to succeed and thrive in a tough real estate market, you need to be extremely good at prospecting and building relationships.

The #1 Best Way to Prospect Is Through Your Community of Influence (COI)

There are various others ways to find new clients too, but let's begin here. Since we all have a circle of people we know, it's time to organize them in such a way you can market yourself as a realtor to them. I'll be honest, when I first got into real estate I didn't want to cold call people. I had no desire, and I didn't think it would work well for me. Since that time the "no call list" has been created making it a possible liability to cold call. When I was new, I started creating a list of people for mailings. It took a few days of brainstorming to find those names and addresses, and it took many hours of concentrated effort.

You Need Two Lists - List A and List B

List A will become your COI list of those you have the closer relationships with. This business is all about relationships so you need to put <u>every</u> friend, family member, business friend, workout friends from the gym, church friends, even your parent's closer friends who know you on the list. Put on everyone you see on a fairly regular basis and everyone who would know you. Make a list of these categories from which to brainstorm. Take time to expand them, writing down all the names, even if you can only remember a first name or a last name. Sometimes you'll write down a last name maybe from a friend of your parents, and then think of their first names a couple of days later. Keep paper with you while you're driving, or watching TV. Keep paper in the bathroom while you get ready in the morning. I thought of names when I'd least expect it, and if I didn't write them down right then I'd quickly forget. Let's begin with family – list your immediate family, then cousins, your parent's cousins, 2nd and 3rd cousins, aunts, great aunts, all your spouse's relatives. Brainstorm until each category is exhausted.

MAKE SURE YOUR CLOSEST FAMILY MEMBERS ARE IN YOUR NAME LIST

The most obvious people still need to be getting your mailings and emails. Your parents and brothers and sisters who seem to be too obvious must be in your list. My dad would say, "Now, stop wasting stamps on me. I already know you're trying to sell houses." But, they need to be reminded what you're doing. As they see you taking this business seriously, so will they. If they don't get your mailings and emails, they might forget to refer you. They might not realize how much effort you're putting in your business if you leave them out of all your marketing. Your closest friends and family are your biggest fans. They will be glad to support you, and as you become successful it will make them feel good to know they helped make it happen. Just a few months ago, my wife's parents were at a neighborhood party. They saw a family they hadn't seen in years, and as they were catching up, those people informed my father-in-law that they were soon hoping to move to Oregon. My father-in-law just happened to have one of my business cards in his wallet. They called me and I listed and sold their house. All along they had planned on using another agent, but the endorsement by my father-in-law was so impressive they called me instead. Make sure you market yourself to your family every chance you can get. They will help you as they can. As you think of various other people's names, don't worry about addresses, just write names. <u>Collect every name you can think of</u>. You can work on getting the addresses later.

BRAINSTORM FOR MORE PEOPLE

List B will have more of the acquaintances and even bulk names from possibly farming neighborhoods. You won't have a very close relationship with people on this list. List B will be much larger than List A by the time you have finished. What organizations have you been in? Chamber of Commerce? Can you get the list from your most recent high school reunion? How about any friends from your brother/sister? Maybe *they* have a recent high school reunion book? How about a church directory? How about a class roster of your kid's class at school? Get *their* parents' names and addresses. Are your kids on sports teams? Get their parent's info too. Even if you only go to the doctor every two years for a physical, that doctor goes in List B with his work address. Try to get names of the front desk people too; they are the ones handling your file. List your dentist and that front desk staff, same with your eye doctor. Have you had a colonoscopy lately? That doctor goes in your List B also just because he literally knows you inside and out. Write down all the possible ways to think of names. Figure out ways to find addresses later, but for now write down every name you can remember. Put paper by your bed at night to write down names and ideas as you think of them. You likely won't remember them after you wake up. Make a concentrated effort to create and expand your List A and B as fast as possible.

I began with the neighborhood where I grew up and looked up every address in the tax records to create my first 200+ names for List B. I should mention at the beginning of my career there was another realtor living in that neighborhood who sold the majority of the homes. She was the queen of the neighborhood and I was about to invade her kingdom. Although I lived in that neighborhood for 25 years growing up, it would be tough to break into her market even with my parents knowing so many neighbors. Still I put every single neighbor in my List B. I joined a local Chamber of Commerce and I included every name and address, unless it was one of the other 30+ other realtors in the directory. All those go in List B. I asked my brother for some of his friends to include so he could be brainstorming. I thought of past coworkers at each job I'd had and I tried to figure out their addresses from tax searches or just using the phone book. Think of previous managers you liked who would remember you. Maybe receptionists and secretaries from those past jobs? I put my dentist, doctors, piano teacher from growing up, anybody I could think of went in my name list. Where are you involved? Who do you see regularly? Are you on committees? All of your current neighbors need to go in list A or B depending on your relationships. Who cuts your hair?

I've always been involved at church. I even met my wife at church. When I first started real estate, I was single and so I asked for a list of names and addresses from my Singles Bible Study class at church. Those went in my name list A because they all knew me. I sang in choir and I got the choir handbook and loaded them in too. I generated over 1200+ names with addresses during my first few weeks as a realtor. It was exhausting, but with enough concentrated effort, you will create a name list too. The problem was none of these people knew I was a realtor. It was a secret to the world. But at least I had a name list.

A few months ago I sent out "football schedule magnets." It has our local Pro Football Team schedule with a Monday night football schedule. Then on the back are some local college football teams, like Missouri, Kansas, Nebraska, Oklahoma, Iowa, etc. The week before I did that mailing, I added nine new names with addresses into my List B just by saying this to total strangers: "You know I'm about to mail out really nice football schedule magnets in a few days. I'd be glad to send you one if you want. They're great to put on the fridge." The key to this is wearing your Realtor nametag to help a real estate conversation occur. These chats will happen in the checkout line at the grocery store. Maybe you're eating at a restaurant with a friend, and the waiter mentions he's thinking about buying his first house. Maybe you're at the gas station and you have your name printed on your windows. A woman comes up to you, "Hey, do you sell houses? Our house has been for sale for three months and about to expire. Our agent has done nothing for us. Would you be interested in coming over to look at it?" Let's say you're at the gym, and you just put on a tank top and shorts. Obviously no nametag. You ask some other person working out, "What do you do that allows you to be here during the day working out?" After he tells you, then he'll ask you the same thing. After it's established you sell houses say, "I'm about to mail out some really nice football schedule magnets. Can I get your address to send you one?" He'll probably say, "Sure, I have some business cards in the locker." Don't make the mistake of letting him leave without getting that contact info. You might never get the opportunity again. Get his card, and give him yours. He'll likely be giving you his work address, and that's fine. Load it into your name list for future mailings and emails. On his business card should be his email address. I would advise sending a very short email saying, "It was nice talking with you at the gym...." Include your website in your email so he can read about you in the meantime if he might be considering moving. The most important thing about your website is that people see your name and picture and have a way to contact you. Remember the bottom line. By now you should have it memorized.

Your COI List Is the Most Powerful Thing You Have in This Business

Make sure you are thinking big enough as to what your COI list (List A) will do for you if marketed effectively. After I met my wife, Carrie, my business was just beginning to take off. It was early in my career and when I proposed to her, 17 months after we met, I asked if I could load all her family and friends into my name list to start sending them mailings too.

Carrie's best friend from college is Christy. At that time Christy was engaged and soon to be married to Louis. She started getting my mailings, and when she and Louis got married I sold them a home. That by itself was a fantastic success story because my COI list worked. Just a few short months after that Louis referred me to a couple of his coworkers which generated another sale. Not too many months after that Christy's grandfather passed away. At that point Christy referred me to her mom who was handling the estate and needed to sell his house. I met with Christy's mom and I got the listing. That house sold to a woman who had her own buyer's agent. She bought that house to fix it up and sell again, but when it came time to relist it a few months later, her agent had quit from lack of sales so she called *me* since I was familiar with the house. She found me from my website after those months had passed. I met with her and I got to list it again. While it was on the market that time, I got a few curiosity calls from potential buyers wanting details on the price. I showed it to one particular family, but they didn't like the house. They did want to see others homes though, but at that time I was so busy with other real estate clients that I referred this buyer to another agent in my office. He was excited to have a new client and gladly paid me a referral fee. After a while this listing sold. While it was on the market, a family called me who lived on the same street as this listing, curious to see how things were going. I was surprised when they decided to move three months later and I listed that house too.

This is an amazing success story, but there's more. The woman who bought that house and flipped it happened to live in a gorgeous home with her husband. He decided to take a job in another city the following year, so they needed to move out of state. She picked me to list their beautiful home after the good job I did staying in contact and developing a relationship during the other transaction. Since that time, Christy and Louis have referred me to other friends and family too. And recently I was able to sell one of Christy's sisters a beautiful new home with her husband, Suzy and Matthew.

If you're brand new, spend some real time creating your list. If you have been in this business for years, then set aside time this week to examine who is in your list. Concentrate on how you can expand both List A and List B. Once you have marketed yourself effectively to your COI list, they will then be referring you to their own COI lists and you've expanded your name recognition to literally hundreds of new people.

Your Friends Can Have Significant Influence on Your Success

I want to tell you about Lorene. Lorene practically took the attitude of adopting me as a grandson when she found out I was selling houses. She had known my parents for over 30 years and had helped my mom when she was going through cancer treatments. She knew my dad well because her own kids were students in my dad's school when he was an elementary principal. After I was out of high school, my family started going to the same church where Lorene went, so I saw her nearly every week for years. Also during that same time I started working part-time at The Jones Store, a local department store since bought by Macy's. Lorene also worked there, so we would see each other there too. She probably even helped me get hired there. Years had passed since I quit working there, but since I saw her at church all the time I sent Lorene my real estate mailings, and she made a point to refer me to everybody she could. One year she referred me to 3 friends of hers, all widows needing to sell their homes to move into retirement apartments. The following year, Lorene herself moved to those same retirement apartments, and I got to sell her personal home. The following year she referred me to her next door neighbor who also moved there. Lorene even referred me to her daughter and her family. That daughter remembered my dad from many years ago as her elementary school principal, so I got to sell their house. She was active in her local PTA since her kids were now in school, and I listed two more homes from her contacts there. A couple of years later, Lorene had her son call me. His wife needed to sell her parents' house. I listed that house, and ended up having a buyer for it. I got to sell it myself before processing the listing papers. In all, Lorene was directly responsible for fourteen separate homes I listed. I wouldn't have known any of these people had it not been for Lorene. She wanted me to succeed, and she worked hard to refer me.

A significant influence in my career has been my friend Mike. I've known Mike since high school. Even though we've both lost a little hair and our waist size has increased slightly over the past 20+ years, we've made a point to keep in contact. I have a close relationship with him after all this time thanks to email and simply making calls every few months just to catch up. In the beginning of my career when I first created my COI list, obviously my closest friends like Mike and his wife went in my list. You might think your friends won't take you being a realtor seriously, but during the first few years of my career Mike referred to me eight clients.

This is what Mike did. He would call his potential client for me *first* to tell them all about me. He built me up to be the greatest realtor in the world to them, and then he would call me.

At that point he had me call the client, and not only did I get my foot in the door by having an appointment, I got to list and sell all eight of those homes.

A few years ago Mike had a coworker mention to him she needed to sell her house. He called me to check my schedule while he was with her, and he set up the appointment for me to go list the house. As I started giving my marketing presentation the client said, "You really don't need to impress me with a presentation. Just tell me where to sign. Mike already told me all about you. If Mike believes in you that much, then so do I." Would you believe that was really just the 5th house I had listed? I wish I had 1000 other friends as incredible as Mike. Between Lorene and Mike, their referrals helped catapult my struggling years into an amazing career.

BECAUSE THIS BUSINESS IS BUILT ON RELATIONSHIPS, YOU CAN MAKE NEW LIFE-LONG FRIENDS

Now, about my friend Lance. Many years ago I was working out at a gym, back when I had a corporate job. Basically I was a peon sitting in a cubicle in a long row of other peons with the peon manager at the end. This was about three or four years before I would get into real estate. I tried to go to the gym right after work to get it over with a few times each week, and there was this guy named Lance frequently working out at the same time. After a while we became friends and helped each other be more accountable to show up regularly. It was good for me to be accountable to someone, since I didn't show up to the gym as often as I should. As time went on we became better friends. We both disliked our dead-end jobs, and shared the common interest of wanting a lot more out of life, and a lot more control of our futures. During the next year I realized my job and the company where I worked were not doing well, so I started looking for another career. That company did indeed end up going out of business. I was frustrated with my lack of income and didn't really have any direction for a new career. I wasn't happy and I needed a change fast. Not wanting to work for anyone again, I started taking real estate classes and got licensed. My newfound flexibility with real estate allowed me to work out at a gym during the day. During that same time, Lance quit his job and got into house/auto Insurance, also giving him flexibility to work out during the day when the gym was less busy.

The flexibility of being a realtor will allow you to set your own schedule. Can you imagine another career offering such flexibility? You can meet friends for lunch and not have the stress of returning to a job quickly. It will also allow you to develop better relationships with your friends, which ironically will be significant to your future income in the business. The following year I started dating Carrie (who became my wife), and Lance and his girlfriend started becoming much more serious. Ironically, we all got married in the spring of 2002. Lance and I were in each other's weddings, and we even spaced mine 2 weeks after his to give him time to return from his honeymoon.

THIS IS WHY IT'S IMPORTANT TO DEVELOP RELATIONSHIPS WITH NEW PEOPLE

Over the years which followed our families both moved to the same suburb and Lance's new career in insurance and mine in real estate give us the freedom to continue meeting at the gym a few times a week. Obviously Lance has become one of my best friends because of the flexibility of my real estate career. My real estate career has flourished also due to *his referrals* and his positive attitude.

Being the recipient of a positive mental attitude from your friends and spouse is vital to your own state of mind. It's part of the awesome power your COI list has. It is the most valuable thing you own. You will develop closer friendships with people, you will have a new freedom and flexibility in your schedule that a 9-5 job cannot give, and you will make money during the process.

MANY OF YOUR FRIENDS ARE WAITING FOR A CHANCE TO HELP YOU

With just a few friends working hard to help you become successful, you can absolutely make a fortune and quickly become a Top Selling Realtor. Ask your friends for help. Ask them for referrals. When Lance gave me names of his closest friends and family, he and I wrote a very short letter that I mailed to all of them explaining he was referring me if they ever needed a realtor. It established a connection so they wouldn't just throw my future mailings away. From that time on, his contacts went in my COI list from that initial referral letter. Many of his friends and coworkers have become my clients thanks to him referring me. In return, I helped market his insurance to all of my new buyers to get a free quote, and many of them are now Lance's customers.

The consistency brought on by your COI list will not only help you succeed in a good market, it will create a foundation to carry you through the times of a tough market too, with fortitude and lasting success.

So again, "How many people know you sell houses?" The fastest solution is to send mailings or emails to the entire name list. Combine both List A and List B to generate labels. The biggest problem with marketing yourself through mailings is the cost, so for my first few years as a realtor, I asked for stamps for my birthday and for Christmas (I asked for stamps for years!) My family didn't want to get me stamps. "What a boring gift," they would say but the times I did get stamps were exciting because I felt like they were investing in my new career. It was especially encouraging my first year, when we all knew I hadn't sold any homes yet.

Let's say you're a new agent with your first listing. What do you do with it? Keep clear notes on prospects. You'll get phone calls from the For Sale sign and emails from the listing online. If you conduct open houses you'll collect even more prospects. Each listing you have is a "lead generator." The reason people have said **"If You List, You Last"** is due to the leads your listings will generate for you if you use them for that purpose. You must be prepared and organized on those phone calls. Memorize the info on your listings: Address, Price, # of bedrooms and bathrooms, which schools they feed into, ages of roof and furnace and A/C. Many times you'll get calls while you're driving, and you need the info in your head to talk intelligently about each of your listings. On occasion your listing will be a good fit for whoever the stranger is on the other end of the call, and so you set up a showing at their convenience. Capture these buyers either for your own listing, or as a buyer for other listings. Find out what they are looking for over the phone to get enough information to know how to proceed. Then either show them your listing that they called about, or tell them you would be glad to pull other houses that better fit what they want. Capture that buyer and sell them a house. Get their email address over the phone so you can start sending them houses online. Then see when you can begin showing them properties. Are they preapproved? They need to be preapproved before you begin or you could be wasting a lot of time. Give them names and phone numbers of loan officers they can call that same day, and then have them call you back to see houses. If they are serious, you'll hear from them again. If not, then you saved yourself some valuable time.

Make sure they're not working with another agent. If they are, then have them call their agent to see your house. Give them all the details on your house and encourage them to see it. Most of the time it seems they are not working with another agent.

"If You List, You Last"

Over time, having your listings generate additional clients will serve as a great way for you to get some quick sales. Sometimes you can show them properties and close on one before the listing they first called you about sells. That's how you work your listings. That's the main reason why people say "If You List, You Last." Just for the record this new buyer only called you because of your listing which came from your COI list. That's how vital your COI list is to your life in this business. A few years ago, a long distance phone company spent millions of dollars marketing their friends and family campaign. They used their existing customer base (which was really their own COI list) to ask them to sign up their friends and family in exchange for promotional pricing. Our new bank may use its growing list of new customers and offer them a free gift for referring their friends and family. Have you noticed this kind of marketing at your own bank from time to time? Maybe you get a free umbrella, or cooler or free screwdriver set if you bring in a friend who opens a new checking account?

If you consistently ask people on your List A to refer you to all their friends and families, you will eventually become a Top Selling Realtor. It worked for me, it works for countless other realtors, and it will most certainly work for you.

#5   WHAT EXACTLY ARE YOU MARKETING?

IT'S YOU. YOU ARE THE PRODUCT. You are the brand. When a person thinks of real estate, you want them to think of you. The buyer or seller believes it's all about them, but they can choose from hundreds of realtors. If you want them to pick you, then "you" is what you're marketing. What can "you" do for them? You need to promote all the good things about yourself to help clients be comfortable with using you. How do you do this with no experience? In the beginning all you can really do is market the real estate company you work for and announce you are a new agent. Promote all *their* positive features. No matter if you work for the largest real estate company in your area or one of the smallest, they are all in business with different advantages. Some offer more technology than others, and the sellers and buyers might have more online tools to help them search for houses. Maybe your company has a name associated with a long tradition of trust in your area, so you can market that. Your broker will have a list of strengths that separate your company from the others. That's where you start. You're developing a brand. You're associating yourself with selling houses, so when the time comes when one of your friends is in her break room at work and her boss mentions they might be selling their house this spring, your friend will say, "If you don't have a realtor yet, I'd highly recommend _____." If you want your name inserted on that line, you need your friend to automatically remember you sell real estate.

THE MORE TIME YOU SPEND ON DEVELOPING RELATIONSHIPS WITH PEOPLE, THE MORE OF A SUCCESS YOU WILL BE

Early in my career I got to show some beautiful, very expensive homes to a young newlywed couple. I didn't get to show houses in this high price range very often, so my wife wanted to come too. Mrs. Buyer was blessed with some inheritance, and Mr. Buyer was blessed with a high paying job, so off we went to find their dream home. We saw winding staircases, lavish master suites, and huge front doors leading to enormous entryways. I knew the husband fairly well from growing up together, but hadn't seen him in years. Because I had loaded his parents into my name list and sent them some mailings, he knew I was in real estate and gave me a call. His parents had referred him to me.

Knowing we were going to look at expensive homes and knowing his wife, whom I had not yet met, was the one with the cash inheritance, I really wanted to make a good impression. I got a hair cut that morning. Then I dressed up, putting on a tie and new dress pants. I even wore brand new black dress shoes. It had snowed that week, a thick slushy snow. Have you ever worn new dress shoes with a slick new sole in the snow? I figured all the homeowners would have shoveled their driveways, but the new construction homes had not been cleared. So we arrived at the 4th house, one of the most beautiful homes I'd ever seen. Even from the street, the palatial estate was something to behold. We barely made it up the ice-covered front steps onto the stoop and I got the key out of the lockbox. We all hung onto each other laughing that if one of us fell, we'd all go down together. I still remember the huge size of the front door with the full-sized windows on each side of it. As I swung open that door, my snow-covered heel hit that slick marble entry floor and I went flying. Both legs went straight up and I was flailing my arms around in a panic trying to grab anything. I landed on my back with such speed that it completely knocked the wind out of me. So there I was lying in my brand new pants, dress shirt, tie and my beautiful brand new black dress shoes … with my wife and this well-to-do couple laughing so hard they were in tears. Afterwards, as Carrie would retell the story, she added the funniest part was the weird dance I did as I tried not to fall. Apparently I made a loud animalistic yelp as I hit the floor. The appropriate reaction on my part would have been to also laugh, and then to get up and shake the whole thing off. But hitting that cold marble floor so hard had left me completely out of breath, and I couldn't talk. I tried to laugh, but unfortunately, I started making weird gasping sounds as I tried to roll over on all fours and catch my breath. Mrs. Buyer pushed me over a bit so Carrie could shut the door while I laid there and recovered. How embarrassing! We looked at 3 more homes that day, and I did sell them a gorgeous home.

Your community of influence needs to begin referring your name. This is how you sell lots of houses. This is how agents work "by referral only". This is how you make your phone ring, and this is how you sell in a tough market.

MARKET YOURSELF TO YOUR COMMUNITY OF INFLUENCE AND THEY SPREAD THE WORD

To summarize: send *mailings* to your COI list, send *emails*, make *phone calls* to them, or see them in person. Seeing them in person continues building a relationship, but seeing your name in print with your phone number reminds them that you sell houses. The advantage of sending mailings is they all get it. Send them a magnet or calendar or ink pen – something they will keep and see repeatedly …especially if the magnet is on their refrigerator. Postcards are less expensive, but often go in the trash with the rest of the junk mail.

Sending emails can have big advantages. They're free to send and easy to type and distribute to unlimited numbers of people.

The disadvantages are that it's difficult to get email addresses for your entire name list as it grows to hundreds of names. It's very easy for them to delete your email before reading it. If they do read it, they'll still delete it so there is little chance they'll see it repeatedly and remember your phone number to pass out. It's possible many of your friends might remember you are selling houses, but have no idea which company you work for or what your phone number is at the moment they need to give it out.

Your COI needs to be reminded you're a realtor however you choose to accomplish it. Sometimes your emails end up going into their spam box because of the number of recipients you're emailing to, and they are never seen or read. You can also send attachments on your emails possibly sending a monthly or quarterly newsletter, but they must open it and read it.

PRODUCTS SELL FASTER WHEN THEY ARE REFERRED TO SOMEBODY ELSE. YOU ARE THE PRODUCT - GET YOURSELF REFERRED

Obviously you need a lot of people knowing you sell houses, but then you need some of them to refer your name to *their* circle of influence. What makes a referral so important is the testimonial they give when they refer you. It's why celebrities and athletes can make millions of dollars a year endorsing a variety of products they might not even use. Cars, shaving creams, clothes, cell phones companies, even hemorrhoid ointments are all referred to you on TV and in magazines by famous people you might recognize. Why do manufacturers pay so much money for these endorsements to have a famous person refer their product? Because it works… and it works big.

When you get *your* COI list referring your name to *their* COI list, your sales will grow fast. There are lots of ways to market yourself to your COI list. How do you market yourself to your COI list effectively while on a budget? Catalogs, marketing companies, expos with vendors, and an entire industry that specializes in taking your money will help you get business. You can buy numerous leads online or have companies create an elaborate website to your liking. You can order postcards to mail out yourself, or you can pay extra for a mailing company to send them for you. Some people scoff at the effectiveness of mailings, but for me they work extremely well. Obviously having a huge COI list is better than having a small one. Let's say you're asking this:

"I Know Size Is Important, But Mine Is Small. What Should I Do?"

You might be sitting there in a panic at this point saying you don't have very many names. For the few names you do have, there is no way to get addresses anymore. You haven't seen those people in years and you also have no money to spend on this business. Understand something very clearly - you can still succeed. If you are a new agent and have no listings and no buyers, do an open house every single Sunday until you get buyers. Be well prepared at your open houses, and over time you will definitely pick up buyers.

You still need a name list though, and size matters. He with the biggest name list wins, or something like that. If you're saying, "I have no friends, and my family won't talk to me", then you might have some issues that this book can't fix. This is a business where it's extremely important that people like you, so invest your time into building relationships with as many people as possible.

#6 You Won't Get Business by Accident.

YOU NEED TO GET YOUR phone ringing with people wanting to sell their current house and buy another. You want first-time buyers to call you personally and say, "My boss at work has your business card, and when I mentioned I was looking to buy my first house, he said to call you, so I'm holding your card right now. What's involved in me buying a house? I hear you're the expert."

You Need Appointments

That is how it works. At that point you have a new buyer. Or somebody calls and says, "Hey we just found out we're having another baby and we need a bigger house before that baby gets here. Can you come over and tell us what our current house is worth? Do you know how we get a loan to buy another?" You need to be getting these calls, generating new leads, and turning them into appointments. It's not enough to be out there just talking about real estate, or sending out postcards, you need appointments. You might find that you get an average of five calls a week just from your current listings asking questions. After you give them the price, they'll usually tell you they need something cheaper. Perhaps you have a listing which is $160,000. You give them the price and they say, "Wow, I really need to stay under $125,000. Do you have any others?" And you say, "YES!" Ask if they are preapproved; usually they are not. See how quickly they plan on buying. First-time buyers are either living at home or renting. If renting, they'll usually be under a lease. Ask when it expires. If they say in two months, then they need to be seeing houses immediately so you can get them under contract with enough time to close. Realize these buyers are calling on numerous other listings checking prices. Don't think they only called on your one property; they might have been calling all week already. Many agents, for whatever reason, do not call buyers back. You could be the first real living agent this potential buyer has spoken with. Have a short conversation asking why they are wanting to buy. Learn their motivation so you can decide if you want to work with them. Basically you're interviewing each other. Within a couple of minutes you can tell if this is going to be worth pursuing. If it sounds good, meet them as soon as possible. First-time buyers have no idea what is about to take place, so setting up a meeting is very important. Begin showing them some houses online to see what their reaction is. Perhaps you have an online system for *them* to be searching for properties. While you're with them, set up the account and have them log in. That way you know they understand how to use it. Set up another appointment to start showing them houses. Have them bring their preapproval letter so you can read what it says and look at their good faith estimate to make sure they are not paying outrageous closing costs. You should have a relationship with some good lenders, so encourage this new buyer to contact your lenders also. That way you can make sure they are really preapproved and look for any red flags that might prevent loan approval.

Capture Your Leads

What does this mean? Your marketing and advertising to find new buyers and sellers consists of emails, mailings, open houses, going door to door in your farming area, and having personal conversations at meetings and clubs, etc. Just because you find out that Mr. and Mrs. Smith are thinking about buying a house, doesn't mean they are going to pick you to be their agent.

Let's say you have done three open houses this month. You've collected 11 names in three weeks. Four of them seemed to be serious buyers. Capture those leads. Who knows how many other open houses they went to? Did you ask if they were already using an agent? If not, offer to help them. As you interview each other, build a quick relationship in the hopes they pick you to help them while they're in your open house. Once they show interest in having you help them, you are capturing them as your lead. If they have a house to sell, offer to go price it for them. If they didn't like the house you had open, then offer to show them others for sale. Find out what their *needs* are and offer to be their solution. You can show them what a really good agent can do for them.

You won't get business by accident. At an open house you have no idea who will walk in the door that day. If a family shows up and they are seriously thinking of moving, then you need to pursue it. If they do not have an agent, they might let you come over and price their home. Don't assume these potential clients will ask you to stop by for tea; you are the one who determines if you meet or not. Sound confident in inviting yourself over. Keep conversations brief and to the point so you get your appointment set up.

Let's say you just mailed out 250 postcards to remind people to reset their clock for daylight savings time. You get a call from somebody on your List B. This is somebody in your mailing list, but you don't know them well. It's a family from a neighborhood you just started farming. You loaded in 150 names and addresses from tax records. So the husband calls you from your postcard. All he wants to know is how much the house next door to him is listed for? You look it up online while he is on the phone with you, and you tell him the price. He might say, "OK thank you", and he hangs up. But maybe while you're logging in, you create a conversation. Ask what he thinks of the house. Maybe ask how this man's house compares to the other one for sale after you read him the remarks. This man may simply be curious and has no intention of moving, but maybe he says, "We'll we've been thinking of moving for a while, and I'm curious what some of these houses are selling for around here. We put in a new furnace this year and we might replace all the windows if we stayed, but I hate to sink too much money into this place if we end up moving." And you say, "I would be glad to pull what every house has sold for around there and drop the info by your house. In fact, I can estimate a price of what your house might also be worth if you want? That way you can decide what to do about those new windows." Don't get too pushy with this because there is a fine line of him being afraid to let you come over for fear of hearing a big sales pitch on listing his house with you. At this point he might say, "Well our house really isn't ready to show and my wife would kill me if I invited a realtor here." You say, "I can easily email them to you. That way you can still get all the info and read about each house that has sold. If that sounds ok, I just need your email address." Guess what, he will be glad to give you his email address. Even though you didn't get an immediate appointment, I bet you're very close to capturing this lead in the near future. After emailing him the comparable homes in the area, follow up with a handwritten note thanking him for calling you and if you can ever provide additional info don't hesitate to call you again. Enclose your business card. After he opens your email and sees the comps, he just might email back and see when you can come over to price their house. That is capturing a lead. You controlled the conversation and started a relationship.

One time I got a call from a lady inquiring about the price on somebody else's listing. It was a cold December night and I was in the middle of watching a movie, but I went to the computer and logged into MLS. I could tell I was on speaker phone and we discussed things like how cold it was outside for her to be driving around calling from different for sale signs while I brought up the listing. This house was priced at $3.4 million! Needless to say, my eyes popped open when I saw the price. At that point I informed her that she needed to be preapproved to be parked in front of a house like that. She informed me they had no idea it was that expensive and how she didn't think they could afford anything in that zip code. We laughed and talked about real estate and what she was really looking for. After a short conversation, I heard hysterical laughter and "Hey Jonathan, this is Jeff. Dude, I'm sorry we got you all excited. We're out here looking at Christmas lights and thought we'd liven up your evening. These houses are huge!" I was naturally a little ticked off since I thought this was a real buyer, but his wife interrupted him, "Jonathan you're really good on the phone thinking on your feet like that. I can't believe you kept the whole conversation going this long. We've been trying not to laugh for five minutes listening to you go on and on! But now I want to buy a house!"

It was three days later and I got a call during the afternoon while I was at the gym working out, "Hello Jonathan, we're parked in front of your listing here in Lee's Summit and we're wondering how fast you can meet us here to let us in?" I responded, "Look, Jeff, it wasn't funny a few nights ago, and it's not funny now. Lunch hour is over and you should get back to work." Well, after another minute of talking I realized these were real buyers and after I apologized I said, "I'm actually just finishing working out close by and if you don't mind me in sweats, I'll be there in 15 minutes." I did meet this family and their kids at the house, but they didn't like it. While I was there I asked for their email address and home address to send them the upcoming baseball magnet. I emailed them some other active homes in their price range, and after a week they emailed back saying they had changed their minds about moving to a larger home right now. I put their info in my name list B, and about two years later I got a call from their kid who had just graduated from college and was getting married. They wanted to buy their first home. I had captured that lead.

Discover their Needs

In order for you to get an appointment determine why people are really calling you in the first place. What is it they want to accomplish? One time I got a call, "Hello Jonathan, this is Sue and we're just wondering if you know of any good roofers?" Jokingly I said, "Wouldn't it be a lot easier to just buy a different house with a new roof?" She informed me they had no intention of ever moving. I said jokingly, "You know the average family moves approximately every five years or so and you guys are raising that average. I think it's time to move." She let me know they didn't plan on ever selling that house, but she made a point to always give my name out to her friends when they talked about moving. I quickly realized she just needed a new roof. It's always a compliment when people call you for advice or referrals, like for a roofing company. It shows they remember you're in real estate and hopefully you can help when they need it.

Are You a Pleasure to Talk with Over the Phone?

Most of your business is conducted over the phone. You can talk from anywhere in your house, or out in the yard, or in another state on vacation. The fact is, when your phone rings be ready to investigate as to why they are calling and what can you do for them.

You're at a public pool, and your four-year old daughter announces to everyone around you that "My daddy sells houses. Who needs a house?" People around you laugh, as if you trained her to say things like that on purpose. A man close by swims over and says, "Do you really sell houses?" I proudly respond in my superhero voice, "Why yes I do." He says, "Well ours has been on the market with an agent for 6 months and it expires next week. We can't stand our agent. She has done nothing for us, and we haven't even heard from her in a month. She probably doesn't even remember she has our house for sale." When this happens I never say anything or interrupt. I let the conversation run its course with them doing all the talking. Secretly I'm hoping he'll want to relist his house with me, but sometimes a seller who wants to change agents can be very hard to please. I don't need another overpriced listing and a high-maintenance seller, so I'll see how the conversation unfolds. In this case he sounds like an okay person, just frustrated. He says, "You know, she mentioned a month ago our house was a little overpriced and we should think about reducing it. We haven't heard from her since though. We'd be ok reducing the price, but at this point we don't want her to be our agent any more. Would you want to come and see if you would be interested in listing our house?" It's time to get out of the pool and get something to write on. Set up an appointment to go view their house.

You need people to be comfortable talking with you so they will tell you their needs. See what currently frustrates them with where they live now. What are their wants and desires? Try to understand their situation by asking questions. Do some investigating to see if you can help them sell or buy a home. The more information you can get from them, the better you can relate and quickly build a relationship. Are they married? Where do they work? What are the ages of their kids? Do they go to church? What are their hobbies? Once you've connected with them, you need to meet with them. Ask when you can see their home. Give them a couple of options that fit your schedule. "I can come over Tuesday or Thursday night? Which is better for you?" You didn't ask if they can meet, you're assuming you're already meeting, so now you just need to know when. You just limited their response from "No we don't want to meet." to "Well how about Tuesday night?" And just like that, you captured this lead.

A couple comes in to your open house, and they clearly don't like it. Maybe it's too much money, or they don't like the floor plan. You start asking a few questions to investigate why they are looking and what they are looking for. They give you a lot of answers and inform you they would have to sell their current home before they could buy another. You offer to meet them to give a price on their current home, but they clearly have no interest in meeting. You even offer to pull other houses for sale they might be interested in, but they don't want you to do that. Not everybody is going to meet with you. You just can't capture all the leads you get. If there is hesitation on having you come over, then try to get their address for a future mailing. Mention you'll be mailing calendars in about a month, and you would be glad to send them one. Maybe you get their address, maybe not. Either way you tried and did your best.

Another family walks in and is looking around. You give them some space to look in peace without you staring over their shoulder, and after they come into the kitchen you say, "Have you been in very many other open houses today?" trying to create some small talk. They don't have much to say. Then you ask, "Is this sort of what you're looking for?" They're trying to keep their kids from touching things in the hearth room, and the wife asks you if there are any houses around there for sale around $300,000? This house is priced at $425,000. If you know the area well, then you can mention some neighborhoods they should see. Offer to show them some other houses or email them what's available. Sometimes people won't give out much information if they feel the agent is becoming too pushy to get it. This family tells you that their old house sold pretty fast and they have just moved into his parents' basement until they decide where to buy another house. If they don't have an agent they're working with, go ahead and get their email address and phone numbers and see when they can meet to see some other houses. Capture them. They likely have no idea where to start with the house-buying process. They need you to take charge in telling them what to do. You won't get business by accident. Become good at leading conversations to the point people are comfortable having you help them. This is how you keep your pipeline full with upcoming business.

USING A QR CODE

A QR Code (abbreviation for Quick Response code) is a bar code that can be scanned using your camera phone and a QR Code Reader. If you have a smart phone or any other phone capable of reading a QR code, download the QR Code application onto your phone and take a picture of the QR Code. You will get directed to the particular web site this QR Code was created for.

For example, this QR Code will take you to my personal web page www.Goforth.ReeceAndNichols.com

"Have a smart phone? Download QR Code app, take a picture and get directed to my personal website!" I print this next to the QR code so people know what it is and how to use it.

CREATE A QR CODE

There are many different websites that allow you to create and monitor QR codes. I created the QR code above by using Google URL Shortener.

First you need to decide what webpage you want clients to go to. Examples might be your personal website, or you can create a different QR code for each of your listings and print it on those flyers. You can even have stickers made for your For Sale signs marketing your personal web page on a QR code. There are companies that also charge for creating codes, especially reusable codes.

Here is how I made the code above:

1. Go to http://goo.gl
2. Click on the Sign In link at the bottom of the page to sign into Google. (Before you create your QR code, you will need to sign into your Google account so that you can monitor the hits on your QR code after it is published.)
3. If you already have a Google account, sign into your account now. If you do not have a Google account, create one now using the "Create an account now" link.
4. Once you are signed in, you should be redirected back to the Google URL Shortener. http://goo.gl
5. Type or paste the full URL of your webpage you want to use in the "Paste your long URL here" box. Make sure to include the http:// at the beginning of your URL. Mine reads: http://goforth.reeceandnichols.com
6. Click the "Shorten" button.
7. You should now see a new entry in your URL list at the bottom of the page. Click on the "Details" link at the end of your URLs row to view your QR code. You should see your QR code in the upper right corner of the screen. You can right click on the QR code and select "Save Image As" to save your QR code to your computer as an image file. Label it, so you know what webpage you linked it to.

MONITOR QR CODES

Once you have used your QR code in your marketing, you will want to know how many times it has been scanned to measure its success.

1. Go to http://goo.gl

2. Click on the "Sign In" link at the bottom of the page to sign into your Google account.

3. Once you are signed in, you should be redirected back to the Google URL Shortener http://goo.gl

4. You should see a list of all the URLs you have created QR codes for at the bottom portion of the page. Click the "Details link" next to the URL you would like to monitor.

5. This page will give you all the information you need to monitor the success of your QR code marketing.

If you flip through a magazine you will see QR codes on many of the advertisements now. You can put your personal webpage QR code on flyers and also put a direct link to the webpage of the listing giving buyers much more information at their fingertips then they ever had before.

If you are unsure how to create a QR code, ask agents or staff in your office for help. They have probably already been making their own.

#7 THE SECRETS OF WHAT I DID AND HOW I DID IT.

THE BIGGEST THING THAT SEPARATED me from many other agents when I was brand new: I treated the opportunity of being a self-employed realtor as a real business.

I TOOK IT VERY SERIOUSLY

I'm amazed how many people get their real estate license just to do it "on the side." They want to piddle around with it and just see what happens. Those people will not last, and they can't make it into a long-lasting career because success doesn't happen by accident. There is a long list of agents who have come and gone in just my office because they didn't take being a realtor seriously. This is a business. Where else can a person become self-employed for such a low initial investment? Have you ever looked into the cost of owning a Subway or a Dairy Queen or a McDonalds? Whatever part of the country you live in, you can spend your money on pre-license courses, and then add the fees to take the real estate exam. In addition to the costs of getting licensed in your state or possibly two states, tack on the fees to join your local Real Estate Board. How much did it cost to sign up with your real estate company and pay their fees (which probably included your business cards, signs, maybe a couple of open-house direction signs, and of course… your nametag)? All of that probably totals less than $4000. At that point you are ready to sell houses with exactly the same opportunity as the most successful agent in your office. Unfortunately, that is where most realtors stop investing in their business. They mail their "new agent" postcards to their COI list, and they text their friends they are a realtor. Aside from that, a few of these agents do an occasional open house over their first few months.

WHY DON'T PEOPLE TAKE THIS INCREDIBLE OPPORTUNITY MORE SERIOUSLY?

A bold statement: In this business it takes money to make money. Being a realtor is expensive because of monthly fees for MLS, your lockbox key, board dues, on and on. But most of your money will be spent on ways to spread the word that you're an agent, and to then spread the word continually over and over and over. You can spend money on continuing education classes and getting designations. If you really want to invest in becoming a success, real estate coaches and trainers have proven systems in place to make you accountable, and to teach you new things to advance your business. All these cost money upfront. You'll also spend a little money on some of your listings, buying flyer boxes to hang on For Sale signs, color flyers to put in the houses, possibly providing lunches for a broker tour on your new listings, and running ads. All of these things cost you money whether that listing ever sells or not. The good news is we're not talking hundreds of thousands of dollars. If you decide to spend $4000 on marketing yourself and your listings this year, you will likely see a very nice return on that investment as people start catching on that you are selling houses.

You have no money to invest into marketing yourself? You can still be a success (as you'll see later in this chapter), but you must get the word out that you're a realtor. You will need to become more effective on the less expensive opportunities: conducting open houses, sending emails, going door-to-door, making calls, etc.

TREAT YOUR BUSINESS LIKE A BUSINESS

If you treat your business like a hobby that might or might not ever come to life then it won't, and you will find yourself in a frustrating career. Among new agents getting started, some will have a full-time or part-time job where they have a regular paycheck, while others will have no other source of income. They will enter real estate as full-time agents with nothing to fall back on. Some will have prepared to enter this business and saved money to invest. At that point the clock will start ticking. How long can a new agent survive trying to become successful, before eventually being forced to quit after running out of money? Some people advise new agents to quit their other jobs so they are forced to work very hard at real estate to survive, others advise new agents to keep their jobs and invest that income into their real estate business. Whatever your situation is, decide to treat this business very seriously and give it the hard work it requires.

From the very first day you get your real estate license, begin doing something every day to reach your goals. At some point you will either be cashing commission checks from selling houses, or you'll run out of money and be forced to examine if you can continue paying your expenses.

Immediately after you get your license, you might not have much to do. You can quickly find yourself with no plan of attack and end up standing around the office drinking coffee with other agents. Instead, use that time productively to learn everything you can.

When I was new, I had a lot of time to take classes and to create a name list. Seize your opportunities to sign up for all the classes you can. Learn the MLS system. Learn about all the online tools your real estate company offers. Take classes on Excel and Word if you don't know how to use them. Get certifications and designations while you have nothing else to do. Gain as much real estate knowledge as you can quickly. My first few months I had no sellers and no buyers. I hadn't sold any houses yet and only 10 people knew I was a realtor. Whether you have a huge name list or very few contacts, you must consistently market yourself to those people. But sending them a quick email that says "Hey, I'm selling houses now," will probably get you no business. Since you can only send out a "New Agent" mailing once, have a marketing plan in place of what you will send out next. Every time you send a mailing, or you email a newsletter, remember it will always be followed by your sending another one.

BRAINSTORM A VARIETY OF IDEAS TO MARKET YOURSELF

Now you need to brainstorm creative ideas to get your name out there. Have an end in sight so your beginning will have a purpose. Sometimes after a few weeks pass with no business, we start second-guessing why we got into this. Educating yourself when you are brand new will speed up your success when your marketing starts working.

Ask your spouse or a good friend to stay up really late and brainstorm with you. Turn off the TV and just talk out loud with no distractions and no phones ringing. Take constant notes. Do you have a catchy last name and might want to think of a corny phrase to help market yourself? Start planning what you're going to do. Have fun with your marketing and think of every far-fetched idea you can. Write them all down. Some of the most ridiculous ideas you will never use will lead to other usable ideas.

DO YOU LOOK LIKE YOUR PICTURE?

The first thing I did as a new agent was get a good headshot picture of myself. Ask your broker to suggest a photographer other agents are using. Then get business cards. Your office will likely make you "New Agent Cards" that you should mail to your name list. Do all this quickly to get your name recognition started as fast as possible. If you are an experienced agent reading this book, get an up-to-date picture of yourself.

I took a listing a few years ago and the buyer's agent had been a realtor since before I was born. I grew up seeing this agent pictured on all of her signs. During the inspection, I stopped by to meet the buyers and to see how things were going on the inspection. I went inside and met the buyers and the inspector and the grandma. After a few minutes I asked where the agent was. The grandma *was* the agent. She looked nothing like her picture! Keep your picture up to date. If you get a headshot taken and really don't like any of those shots, go to another photographer that same week. You will need a couple of other shots of yourself too. Get a good picture standing with a For Sale sign that says SOLD perhaps, especially if your picture is on your signs.

No Money to Invest? Begin with Going Door-to-door

Headshots don't cost very much, especially if you use a photographer other agents are already using. Marketing yourself, however, costs more. Let's say you have little money to spend on mailings. An idea would be to "farm" a certain neighborhood by walking it with flyers or door hangers. You can walk the streets for free and put door hangers at each house, if there are no anti-soliciting laws in place there. I went door-to-door hanging flyers for over a year until I got too busy to spend the time walking. Some of those flyers probably blew off in the wind, and some homeowners might see this as an unprofessional way of marketing yourself, but it can work and the exercise doesn't hurt either. Another disadvantage to putting flyers door-to-door is most people enter through the garage, and might rarely open their front door. It might rain for two straight days before they see your flyer wadded up on their doorknob, but still it's a very inexpensive way to get your name out there.

IT TOOK ME A WHILE TO RESORT TO THIS

I had been sending mailings to the neighborhood where I grew up and for many months holding open houses on other agents' listings, when I decided to go door-to-door. Have you thought about farming an area by going door-to-door? Maybe you just want to walk and put flyers on doorknobs, but not actually knock. Why would an agent be afraid to knock? Because we really don't know what to say? I did <u>not</u> want to go door-to-door. My dad nagged me to the point I finally did it because he said I was around the house too much and other agents kept listing houses in the neighborhood instead of me. I put a big wad of rubber bands in my left pocket, and carried a flyer or a magnet in my right hand. I walked up and rang the doorbell. Most of the time nobody came to the door anyway, but I had to have some scripts memorized just in case someone would answer the door. Some people were outside raking leaves or washing cars. Some adults were on the driveway playing with their kids or unloading groceries. My goal was to talk to at least one person while out walking, so I decided I might as well knock on all the other doors along the way. A flyer offering a "free market analysis" of their property, or giving them a baseball schedule magnet made it easier.

If I am going door-to-door today, I ring the doorbell. When they open the door looking irritated I'll say, "Hi my name is Jonathan Goforth. I'm a realtor with Reece & Nichols and I'm going door-to-door today handing out free baseball schedule magnets. If you ever hear of anyone wanting to buy or sell a house, I hope you pass along my info." Sometimes they'll just take it and say "Thanks." Sometimes they'll say, "Hey years ago I went to college with a Goforth back in Texas. I wonder if you're related?" Then I laugh and say, "I doubt it but I guess if we go back far enough we'd be related." And they say, "Thanks" and shut the door. On occasion they say, "You know, my sister and her husband are looking to buy a house. I don't know if they have an agent yet or not, but I'll give them this."

SUGGESTIONS FROM MY DAD

My dad advised, "Never, never, never walk on their grass. Always go back down the front steps down the driveway to the street and then up the next driveway. Never wear shorts or jeans even if it's hot out." (I always wore dress pants with a dressy shirt). Make sure your flyer is professional, because the product you're selling is you. Always be professional and courteous. Hand them your flyer or magnet with it face up and turned in the direction so they can read it. Don't have your name at the top of your flyer; your name should be at the bottom in big letters with your picture and phone number. You'll be holding the flyer at the top, so don't let your thumb cover your name. Your flyer will probably be in the trash within ten seconds so you want them to see your name as long as possible. Many times people are not home, so I rubber-banded the flyer on their doorknob. I did this monthly for 9 months in my original farm neighborhood. Do you know how time consuming that was? Did it work? Yes - *eventually*.

Dad always said, "If you get asked in somebody's house along the way, remove your shoes in the entry way. Even if you know your shoes are clean, it's a sign of respect. If the homeowner says it's fine to leave them on then you have their permission." These potential future clients will remember how serious you take your job and the care you give their home.

THE POWER OF REPEATED ADVERTISING

What makes advertising successful is repetition, building on itself to develop name recognition. If a soda company can spend millions of dollars to advertise for 30 seconds on TV, then a neighbor holding your flyer for 10 seconds is priceless. If you're going to farm a neighborhood by walking house to house, then make a commitment to do it repeatedly, sending occasional mailings and emails too. Farming an area takes a big commitment to do it correctly. I spent countless hours hanging flyers on doorknobs, and most of the time I'd ask myself "Does this even work? I walked that neighborhood (approximately 300 houses) over and over and over. Ask yourself, "How badly do I need to succeed?" If I can't spend money on mailings to these people, then what other options are there to spread the good news faster that "I am a realtor?"

WHAT SUCCESS DOES THIS BRING?

The first time I went door to door, I got no calls. None from the second, or the third time either. At that point, I was considering quitting completely. The fourth time I got a call, but they only wanted me to estimate the value of the house because they were thinking of refinancing it. The fifth, sixth, seventh and eighth time – nothing.

The ninth time I walked the neighborhood, I got a call and finally listed a house. I skipped the tenth month because I was sick and tired of walking. I heard another agent in my office mention how she got a listing from going door to door in her neighborhood so I started again. I did it four more months with my dad walking the other side of the street to help out. One time we were putting flyers on doors near the top of Dad's street, and he yelled over to me from across the street at the top of his lungs, "Now Jonathan, Mrs. Alexopolous here is going to be moving next spring! She wants you to come over here and look at her house and see what she needs to be doing! Think you can come over here?!"

During those last four months I got two more listings. One of those listings sold quickly and it was wonderful to get a commission. The other house took longer before selling, but while it was for sale I got calls from prospective buyers. A husband and wife let me show them the house. They didn't like it so I asked if I could show them other homes as their buyers' agent. They agreed and I sold them a different home two months later. They referred me to Mrs. Buyer's brother, and to her boss a year later when he needed to list his house and buy another. I'm glad I went door to door all those times, because long-term profitable results were just getting started.

FARMING WITH AMERICAN FLAGS

The real estate company I work for offered for us to buy small professionally made American Flags on wooden sticks with a note attached. My name and phone number on the note wished them a happy 4th of July, and it encouraged the homeowner to call me if they were considering selling their home. I ordered 300 of them my 3rd, 4th and 5th years in the business and placed one along the street at each driveway in the neighborhood I was farming. An impressive sight over 4th of July weekend! Did I get business off that? Yes. This is the same neighborhood where I sent mailings and went door to door, so there was a compounding effect of marketing to keep my name in front of them.

When I began farming this neighborhood, another agent was listing the majority of everything for sale in that whole area. She had it wrapped up and I knew it would be difficult competing against her. Other agents had listed houses consistently in there too. Since I began farming that neighborhood (even with the slow success in the beginning), I have listed and/or sold 41 homes there. Along the way I made a rider for the top of the For Sale signs stating "Neighborhood Specialist." The year I sold more houses in that neighborhood than the woman who had it all locked up for years, I knew I had arrived. It was great! That one fantastic year was a turning point for my business in that area, and I sold even more the following year. Many of those 41 clients have referred me to even more clients.

SUCCESSFUL MAILINGS

The <u>most important thing</u> is that your mailings get opened. How often do you go through your own mail and throw things away without opening them? You need to make sure your mailings are always opened by 100% of those to whom you are mailing. How?

I preprint my return labels in color ink, but the clients' name and address is hand written. Your spouse will likely help if you have hundreds of mailings to address. If you're mailing Postcards, then labels are fine since there is nothing to open. You'll find out quickly there are many companies who specialize in mailings. They will make you customized postcards and even mail the postcards to your COI list for you... at your expense.

Here is what I did my first two years. I sent out a mailing to 1000 people nine months out of the year for three years. I mostly sent postcards because they were cheaper and faster for sending huge mailings. I mailed them myself by printing my own name list on labels putting them on the postcards with stamps. That way I would also get them returned if anyone had moved and needed to be removed from my list. I could get an entire mailing done in 3 nights while watching movies. I sent recipe postcards, baseball schedule postcards, city events schedule postcards, Happy 4th of July postcards, football schedule postcards, and time-change reminder postcards in both spring and fall, etc. My 2nd year as a realtor I bought bulk recipe cards for four separate mailings, but one featured a gourmet shrimp-coconut dip, and I thought "uh oh" this postcard will go in the trash instantly. When I took my first two listings, I had the front picture of those houses made into custom postcards to show off my new listings. These mailings weren't cheap because they were customized postcards, but it was the fastest way I knew to get my name out there consistently. That custom postcard did generate some calls but unfortunately I still wasn't getting much business. It appeared most of the postcards I was sending out were going in the trash so fast they probably didn't even notice my name. I should have been mailing something that was worth reading, and worth keeping.

MY BIG MAILING OF THE YEAR

What worked for me might not work for you. Some agents will tell you that mailings don't work and are too expensive and they don't do them. Examine those agents to see (1) how successful are they, (2) if they are successful, what did *they* do to get business? Successful agents all did something to market themselves in the beginning. Chances are what they did is listed in this book. No matter what you say you're going to be doing, there will be a few negative agents who will criticize you for doing it. You'll hear, "Don't do open houses. I haven't had a good open house in two years. They just don't work anymore." Or, "Why are you wasting your time going door-to-door? You're not going to get business that way." Or, "You're ordering 500 calendars? Do you know how much that costs? You've got to be crazy!" Don't listen to advice from unsuccessful agents. Do everything productive you can to get your name out there.

The real estate company I work for offers Kansas City Calendars we can purchase each year. Professionally made, they show 12 seasonal pictures of Kansas City landmarks. They don't cost too much individually, but for large quantities it gets expensive. Sending calendars is the most effective mailing I do. Why? Because it stays up all year, and clients look at it nearly every day. I've ordered them now for the past 9 years, and clients have come to expect them. If your company doesn't offer something like this, then brainstorm ideas of other things you can mail that clients will keep.

One year I even bought bulk Valentine's Day cards and sent those with my business card. Another creative mailing is to buy cheap flower seed packets of "forget me nots" to mail in the spring. Keep in mind I needed 1000 of them, so I spent two days driving to every Wal-Mart, Lowe's and Home Depot to buy all their seed packets. I included a catchy flyer so they wouldn't forget I was in real estate with the "forget me not" seed packets. Did that mailing work? Yes. In fact it worked so well, that I did it in March two years in a row – great timing going into the busy Spring market.

Most agents in my office don't spend as much as I do on mailings, but in recent years I have listed more homes than any other agent in my office – as an individual agent. I spent more money on mailings my first three years because I had to get my name out there fast. The monthly mailings I did in the beginning created a foundation that took longer than I expected. But once I had consistent business, I backed off some of the mailings. I don't spend nearly as much now as I did my first few years in the business. As my income has risen, my expenses have dropped.

MARKETING THROUGH EMAILS

When I was a new agent many other realtors sent mailings. As the internet became more popular for mass emailing, most agents cut back on snail mail due to the cost. For me, traditional mailings became more effective as E-marketing took over for other agents. Four years ago, I realized that I too could save a fortune if I could get into the E-Marketing with everybody else. The problem? At that time I had a name list with over 1000 names and current addresses, but with only 127 email addresses. Some of the agents in my office created a custom post card to mail to get emails addresses with the enticement for their names to be included in a drawing for a large gift certificate. We all chipped in a little money toward this giveaway. Thinking it would work well, we would each collect email addresses for all of our COI lists. Would you believe I only gained 47 more emails?

This was at a time when most real estate companies were coming out with new ways to Electronic-market ourselves to our customers, by sending them E-flyers for each occasion. Some of these E-marketing programs cost money to subscribe to, but it was a lot cheaper and faster than mailings. As E-marketing became popular, even I was getting solicited by numerous other realtors who had my email address asking to sell my home. That year I received 19 identical Happy St. Patty's Day E-Flyers from different agents all using the same E-marketing system. I quickly learned how to delete spam.

If you are going to concentrate entirely on E-Marketing, make certain you have your entire Name List A and Name List B with active email addresses. Should you market yourself to your COI through emails? Yes! Send emails that are creative enough to get opened, but don't limit yourself to just internet marketing. I didn't see how E-Marketing would help me succeed with the same effectiveness as mailings, so I continued with regular mailings to my entire name list too.

Consistency Is Crucial

In addition to hand addressing your mailings, sending emails, and going door-to-door, you need to send some communication consistently. If you're sending a postcard, chances are it only gets looked at for a few seconds before it goes in their trash. But the more of your mailings they see, the more they will remember your name and what you do. It will take six months of mailings before you will likely see any results. Earlier I mentioned a statement by Rich Casto that is so powerful I want to mention is again, "If you touch a prospect 6 times, then 85% of them don't have a choice but to remember you." Think of TV and how many times a company shows the same commercial.

Going into my third year as a realtor my sales *finally* started to increase, and I realized I was spending a lot of money on mailings, but I still wasn't selling very many houses. I looked at the monthly postcards I was sending out – recipes, "Happy 4th of July", etc. They had worked to a degree, but I felt like the few seconds they were noticed before going in the trash might not be very cost effective. So I started doing only 5 mailings a year to my COI List, and also sent "Just Listed Cards" to many of the neighbors around my listings.

JUST LISTED POSTCARDS

Rich Casto also says, "The 2nd biggest source of getting listings is through Just Listed Cards." In my fourth year I committed to sending postcards advertising my new listings to neighbors surrounding each new listing. I also sent "Just Sold" cards to households surrounding each of my sales. Jumbo-sized custom postcards from a local mailing company showed a full-sized picture of the front of the home, with my picture in the corner on the front *and* back, along with my name and phone numbers. I also gave 50 unaddressed postcards to the homeowner for them to pass out to their friends and at work.

At that time I had listed two beautiful homes I wanted my entire circle of influence to see. It was a life statement announcing that I had finally arrived and had listings. One was a beautiful cape cod, with a great picture. The front of the home had great curb appeal and created a really sharp looking mailing. It simply told people about my new listing and encouraged them to call me for a free market analysis of their property. The front of the postcard said *"Another Home Just Listed by Jonathan Goforth."* I still remember those postcards and how proud I was. It was a powerful statement because not only was I reminding them I was a realtor, but now I had proof I was selling houses. Clients want to use an agent who has experience and who is successful. "Just Listed" cards give you the credibility your clients want to see, while branding yourself not just as a realtor, but a *successful* realtor. It was my goal to send 100 "just listed" cards for each new listing, if that listing was in a neighborhood where I wanted more business. Did it generate new business every time? Of course not, but with consistency it started paying off.

A few years ago I sent out 100 "just listed cards" around a new listing. I got a call from an elderly couple a block over who wanted to move to California to be closer to their kids. I had never met these people before, but when I arrived at their home, the husband was holding my "Just Listed" card. Mr. Seller said in a loud voice "Young man, I'll tell you right now I can't hear well so you're going to have to talk loud!" So I talked loudly the whole time we looked through the house. Along the way his wife, who was also hard of hearing, joined us on the tour. We sat at the dining room table as they told me all about their grandkids in California. I learned so much about their grandkids that I felt like I had grown up with them. The funny thing was they both talked as loud as possible the whole time constantly interrupting and correcting each other. When it was time to fill out the disclosure, Mrs. Seller filled it out because she could read more easily. She read each question slowly and as loudly as possible. Mr. Seller yelled numerous times," What? Speak up dear!" Four hours later (making this the longest appointment I'd ever had) they were really getting on each other's nerves, correcting each other about the age of the furnace, appliances, etc. I still remember to this day how hot they kept their home. Near the end of the appointment, I remember sitting there sweating wishing they would hurry up. As my voice was starting to get hoarse from yelling everything I was saying to both of them, they got into a discussion about the age of the roof for the Disclosure. Mrs. Seller read the question as loud as she could to her husband, "How old is the roof?" He replied with a familiar response, "What?"

"I said, how old is the roof?" she yelled back. As he paused and looked up towards the ceiling rubbing his chin, she yelled even louder, "I said, How old is the roof?" He yelled just as loud, "I heard you the first time, I'm thinking!" Then she got up and went in the kitchen to get some water. He yelled as loud as possible so she could hear in the kitchen, "I think it was back in 2006 when I had that vasectomy, cause the doctor thought it would be a good idea." I had to cover my smile as I sat there. "Dear, didn't we get the new roof that same week?" He pointed at me as he said in the same loudness, "Have you had a vasectomy yet? They make me have a vasectomy every five years just to check! My doctor is good at vasectomies! I've never felt a thing!" At this point I was openly laughing pretty hard. He continued yelling, "I get my next one when I turn 90 next year. Last time I nearly crapped myself the night before getting ready though!" Mrs. Seller walked back in with glasses of water, "You had a colonoscopy! Not a vasectomy!"

"What???"

She yelled as loud as possible with her voice cracking, "Colonoscopy!"

My point with this story is that "just listed" and "just sold" cards can work if the card is well designed and sent consistently.

WHAT TO PUT ON YOUR FLIERS

How can you keep flyers and emails from being boring? If you get awards in your office, let everyone on your List A and List B know about it. Maybe you listed three houses that month. Do a mailing or email with the pictures and addresses of each house so people in your name list can see your accomplishments. Success will breed more success. After selling a house, make a flyer with a picture of the house with a testimonial from the sellers. Keep it short and simple so people will read it. As your COI repeatedly sees this kind of powerful marketing from you, you'll be amazed at the speed you brand yourself as a successful realtor to them.

If you ever wanted to be famous or have a little attention, this business will give you that opportunity in your community to some degree. If you want to see your name up in lights, then get your name in as many people's front yards as possible. It's fun to drive by your listings just to see your name and, believe me, that wonderful feeling never gets old. Right now my three kids are ages 4, 2, and 1. The oldest kids yell "Daddy! Daddy! Daddy!" when we drive by one of my listings because my picture is on all my signs. Wouldn't it be great if we could get the general public to get that excited when they see our For Sale signs?

The same time I stopped doing monthly postcards, I started making my own flyers to mail out instead. It was time consuming but effective to make my mailings personal. I sent a Happy New Year's mailing, a very short personal letter mentioning what was going on in my life and thanking them for their support. I also advertised I would give a free market analysis of their property. At a motivational seminar a speaker suggested making a little certificate advertising a "Free Market Analysis" of their property. So for all my future mailings I made a little slip (a third of the size of a sheet paper), cut them out, and I included those slips in two mailings a year. Talk about making the phone ring! I would get numerous requests for me to come and price houses. It generated future business for my pipeline and started giving me confidence in my ability to have a lasting career. Make sure you get things like this approved by your broker. There is required information that has to be on every mailing sent out. I have sent a Happy Valentine's flyer mailing over the most recent years, but I no longer send Valentine's cards because I feel I can make a less expensive flyer that's more personal. If your busiest season is spring, like it is in the Midwest, then send more flyers in January, February and March. You need to list as many houses as possible in the early spring to maximize your income.

If you have a baseball team in your city, then you might send out magnetic baseball schedules. I used to send a postcard schedule, but I now send a more professional plastic schedule with a magnet on the back, designed to fit in an envelope. After I started mailing out these refrigerator magnets, my business really started to climb. Instead of my postcard going in the trash after 5 seconds, it now went on their refrigerator for months. My next mailing is early August for the football schedule. Again, another refrigerator magnet. I also put a flyer thanking them for their support. My wife and I began having kids four years ago, and for most of these flyers my kids are pictured doing something with us. Most years we all get dressed in football clothing for a football mailing picture, and the same for the baseball mailing. Do a patriotic picture for the summer mailing. Do an Olympics theme advertising you're a winner, or going for the gold in selling their house, etc. Get creative. The more consistent you are with creative mailings, the more people will enjoy opening them up. In the fall I've done "Back to School" mailings, Thanksgiving mailings, and then in December we send the Kansas City Calendar through bulk mail. Inside the calendar is another flyer wishing them a Merry Christmas with a picture of my family. The last two years have been busy, even in a tough market, so now I only send a Valentine's mailing, baseball schedule magnet, football schedule magnet, and the calendar. Just four mailings. Do they work? Yes! And in a huge way.

Another opportunity for a mailing is to announce when you obtain professional designations. You know what these are – the letters you can put after your name, like ABR, CRS, GRI, etc. Your clients really don't care what the letters stand for (most agents don't even know what these letters stand for) but they give you credibility. We all enjoy having letters after our names. It makes us feel confident and important. Does it get me business? To tell you the truth I have no idea, but it certainly doesn't hurt. I just like having some letters, and it makes for a good mailing.

NEWSLETTERS

If you want to go the extra mile, create a newsletter. You can use the same format each time, and just change the articles. Include specific housing information about their neighborhood, or generic housing data provided by the National Assoc of Realtors. Give an update from a lender on your newsletter. Give updates on your current listings and how many houses you've sold recently. You can even print a calendar on the back listing various events going on in your city. That might be a great reason for them to keep your flyer. Put in pictures of your family. The better you create some feeling of a relationship on paper, the more likely future clients will want to use you. Put a useful recipe of the month, or when daylight savings time starts, etc. Monthly or quarterly newsletters can either be mailed or emailed. Remember: your goal isn't to drown your clients with useless information; it's only to spread the word that you're a realtor.

YOUR WEBSITE

Do you have a website? You need one. The real estate company you work for probably has already set one up for you. It doesn't have to be fancy or cost much money if you customize it, but you must have one. Advertise your website on every single piece of marketing along with your name and phone number. Mailings, flyers, calendars, magnets, even your car windows. If I could get by printing it on my forehead I would. Your company has probably already made you a generic site and it probably already links any listings you might have. Most of what is on there probably can't be changed, but if you can personalize your site then you can answer a question that all potential clients want to ask you... Why should you be their realtor? You want people to visit your site and read about you. The more times they see your name and face the more you're creating a brand with them. Take advantage of your tech department and have them help you customize your website. They can also refer you to people who can do it for you inexpensively. How seriously you take your website shows how seriously you plan on making it as a realtor. If your website doesn't stand out from all the other agents in your office, neither will you.

THIS IS PERHAPS THE ONE PLACE YOU'RE SUPPOSED TO BRAG ON YOURSELF

It's YOUR website. It's your resume and it's who you are. Put everything relative to real estate and anything personal you don't mind the whole world knowing. Talk about your family. Talk about your experience. List the organizations you belong to. List reasons why a potential client should use you. Make sure you have testimonials on your website, and take pictures of the clients in front of their houses standing next to your customized For Sale sign saying SOLD. Potential clients looking at your site or seeing your mailings should see other satisfied clients to give you credibility. Your tech department can help you link other sites to yours such as various school districts' web sites, your local zoo, news channels, local weather, mortgage companies, etc. The more value your website can offer your clients, the more likely they will look up your site.

LISTING PRESENTATION BOOK

You need something to carry into your listing appointment that will (1) make you look professional. (2) set you apart from your competition. Your listing presentation book will have sections which will always be the same. You can simply print this out for each presentation in advance. There will be a section about you, and a section about your company. Other sections will explain the importance of RELO, and charts and graphs showing your market share as a company. You will also need a CMA customized for that particular home also in your book. Put all this in a professional looking leather binder, possibly even embossed with your name on the front. If you are simply being interviewed that night then leave your book with them.

Some agents walk in with a lap top and show their presentation on slides using the computer screen. Whatever method you choose to present yourself, make sure you are professional and concise. Don't leave them a 200 page book. Your company will likely have various marketing pages you can pick and choose from to create your book. Create a customized sheet about you to put at the front. You can add another page showing pictures of your past listings to give you credibility. Advertise your awards and certifications. Tell your potential client why they should choose you and the company you work for to sell their home.

CUSTOMIZED FOR SALE SIGNS & DIRECTIONALS

As you get busy and start listing numerous homes, invest in customized For Sale signs, with your name, picture and website as large as you can get it printed. Obviously your broker has to approve any changes you make to your signs, but your company might already offer customized signs at your expense. If you plan on becoming a strong Listing Agent, then this is a must. Find out the cost, and budget it in early. Have you noticed the most successful Realtors have their picture on their For Sale signs? In the neighborhood where I grew up, after I started selling a few houses, I had five listings within three blocks of each other at one point. I started putting "Neighborhood Specialist" across the top of those customized For Sale signs as I mentioned earlier. What did that do? It got me even more listings!

Another way to get your name out there is to order "Open House Directionals" and "For Sale Directionals" with your name printed across the top. Many cities do not allow you to put "For Sale Directionals" on city easements, so find out whether they are allowed in your area. Even if they are allowed you'll still get many stolen, but you'll find them to be a great way of getting more name recognition… *if* your name is on the sign.

BECOME A DRIVING BILLBOARD

A few years ago I put my name, phone number, website and company name on my SUV's windows. I did the sides and back glass. The good news is that people will see your name everywhere you go. The bad news is that people will see your name everywhere you go too. I have to be careful how I drive. It's no longer acceptable to cut people off, I can't really speed, and it would not be advisable to park illegally in a handicapped space! I would never do that anyway, but I'm saying if your name is plastered all over your vehicle, people are watching.

Honking at pedestrians is not wise and I have to use the carwash more often to keep my name clean. A personal comment, if you have your name plastered all over your car too much, people are probably laughing. Some agents must have giant-sized egos, but at least they get noticed I guess. My name and number are very simply done, but large enough to be seen. Any sign company can probably do it for you.

Just two months ago, I was at a gas station putting air in my tires. A car pulled up next to me. They rolled down their window and said, "Hey, do you want to sell our house?" This is usually where I'm thinking I'm on candid camera and the whole thing is a prank. I played along as I walked over to them and said, "Sure." They informed me that they had seen my For Sale sign in their neighborhood earlier this year and their house was currently for sale, but they were really unhappy with their current agent and never seemed to hear from her. After their listing expired, they said they would call me so I handed them my card. Would you believe I listed their house two weeks ago and have it for sale right now?! I firmly believe you should make yourself a driving billboard.

ADS IN THE NEWSPAPER

The most expensive waste of advertising money for me was placing ads in the <u>Kansas City Star</u> newspaper. This is the largest local newspaper and it even had regional inserts to advertise cheaper to certain geographical areas. The regional sections had local news and articles about schools and businesses, so I thought that would be the perfect way to target where I was already starting to sell houses. I remembered from marketing classes in college that an advertising campaign really needs to run for a minimum of 6 months before checking its effectiveness. It was my fourth year of selling houses, and I decided I would take some of my income and make myself an overnight success by placing ¼ page ads in the newspaper. I ran professionally-designed ads every other week for 6 months. I'm not sure how many new clients I needed to be able to call the ad campaign a success but I thought enough new business to pay for the ads would be ideal. After 6 months, I got zero calls. None. Talk about depressing! I had wasted a lot of money, but at least I tried and gave it a good strong effort. I'm not saying it won't work for you, but it sure didn't work for me.

HANDWRITTEN THANK YOU NOTES

I've consistently mailed handwritten thank you notes to people who came to my open houses. It's time consuming but gives that extra touch after an open house is finished. I did it the first year I was a realtor because I had nothing else going on, and I heard at a real estate seminar it was a smart thing to do. I've picked up listings and also many buyers from following up with prospects coming through open houses. I had an open house and the neighbors a block over were out walking and stopped by to see how the house compared to theirs. I followed up with a thank you note and my business card, as I had done probably a hundred other times over the last couple of years. These people called me and I did list their house. In fact, I listed and sold their house before I sold the house they came to see. That first year of consistently handwriting notes put me in the habit of doing so all the time. It's easiest to take thank you notes with you and write them during the last 30 minutes you're at the open house, then they're ready to mail.

ADVERTISING IN YOUR CHURCH

If you are active in your church see if there are any opportunities to advertise. Is there a church directory? Maybe a weekly newsletter or bulletin? If many people attending that church are in your community of influence you need to be advertising there. If you have very little money to spend, then at least get a small ad in place. Start with a business card sized ad. You'll find there are likely other realtors advertising too. See if you can get yourself up to a ¼ page ad or larger to make it more noticeable. It's important for you to realize if you have a realtor in your church who gets all the clients and you know there is really no way to break into that market now, you are not thinking big enough. Many times things appear to us only as they are at that moment, but we forget to look into the future. Maybe that agent gets all the business because there aren't any other realtors to call. Once you get a happy client, they will start spreading the word and next thing you know you are selling quite a few houses. My family attends a large Baptist Church and it has almost no advertising opportunities, so I've had to collect as many names and addresses as possible to put into my Name List A or Name List B to spread the word.

Some people feel uncomfortable when marketing themselves to their church friends because of how it can be perceived. Here is what I have noticed: If you can do your marketing tastefully then you need to let people know you are a Realtor. If you are active in your church then you should know people who will be entered in your Name List A. If your church is small, you might know most everyone in your church on a first-name basis, but if your church is large you'll be entering most of your names in Name List B just because you don't know them well. First Baptist Church in Raytown, where we attend is a huge church, and it's impossible to know everyone. Even our choir is enormous. I was in choir for years before I even thought about real estate so I already had many relationships in place, but on occasion somebody would join the choir and immediately solicit themselves aggressively to everyone. It was not well received.

We had a loan person join once who was so "in your face" about using her that it really turned most people off. There are dozens of other realtors in this same church too. My wife and I were involved at church long before I got into this career so we didn't join a church only for the purpose of networking to advance a career. If somebody joins a group at church with the ulterior motive of getting business then people will see through that fakeness immediately. If you are already involved in your community and your church with relationships in place, then you should advertise yourself to those people. Let them know you are a real estate agent.

JOINING A CHAMBER OF COMMERCE

Joining a Chamber of Commerce will only work if you become active. Attend as many socials and luncheons as possible. I've been a member of three Chambers in areas where I now sell a lot of property. Surprisingly, I never gained a single client from the Chambers. I would think they can be a great source of business, but it depends how many other realtors are already involved and how much time you can spend attending functions. Functions can also be expensive. If you've always wanted to become active in your community by joining your local chamber, then now is your opportunity. Use the flexibility of your new schedule and make all the friends you can at those Chamber events.

JOINING A GYM OR FITNESS CENTER

A local fitness center can be a good place to gain clients; it's also good for your health and appearance. I have sold houses to four people I met from working out. One of them was a friend from high school and we hadn't seen each other in years. We happened to be working out at the same time and caught up one day. I gave him one of my business cards. Not too long afterwards he and his wife bought a house from me. They also referred me to 3 other families.

NEIGHBORS

Neighbors are a great source of businesses. How well do you know your immediate neighbors? Do they all know you sell houses for a living now, or are you waiting to tell them *after* you become a success? They are probably wondering why you're home all the time! Make sure they all get your mailings and emails because they all know other people.

COMMUNITY OF INFLUENCE

The ultimate purpose of your COI List is to have them refer you to *their* friends and family. If you only have 50 names in your community of influence, but just 10 of them refer you to another 5 names, you have 50 brand new names. Your closest friends might not feel comfortable using you as their realtor in the beginning. Nobody wants to be your first customer. Why? You might screw the whole thing up and they will regret they picked a friend with no experience. It's hard to fire a friend. I've been amazed that my closest friends had no problem referring me to their other friends instead. In fact as I mentioned earlier, some of my friends worked as hard as I did to establish my business. Anytime you get referred by someone you need to go the extra mile to make sure that customer is thrilled they picked you. The person who recommended you has stuck their neck out by referring you. When they hear what a great job you did, they will not only be relieved but will most definitely give out your name again – and the client you just helped will also be giving you referrals too. If you're going to become a consistently successful agent year after year, you must get your community of influence to send you referrals. The more people who know you sell homes, the more homes you will sell.

Never Remove People from Your COI List

You'll be tempted to remove people from your name lists over time because you never hear from them, especially from List B. I still have most of the neighbors where I grew up in my List B from farming that area, but I haven't spoken with many of them in over 15 years. Frustration sets in after years of mailings to certain people I've never heard back from. When it comes time to order expensive magnets or calendars and I see how much money it costs, my instinct it to eliminate names from the list to shrink it down. The problem is which names should I eliminate? You never know when you will get a referral from somebody you haven't seen in years and then you are thankful you sent them that most recent mailing. My personal rule is – never ever remove somebody from the mailing list. Never. If you have names and a current address, keep mailing to them.

Your HOA Newsletter & Directory

If you live in a neighborhood with a Home Owners Association, ask about advertising opportunities. My HOA has a neighborhood's newsletter which I've advertised in consistently. It comes out every three months and I run a half-page ad in it. Unfortunately I'm not the only realtor running an ad, but I have to make sure my neighbors know I sell houses, and so do you. It's not about hoping they might move away so you can sell their homes; it's really about wanting them to refer you to *their* COI. Have them refer you to *their* aunts, uncles, cousins, friends and coworkers. Think BIG when it comes to using your name list. Have a plan to consistently get your name out there, whether it's doing open houses, hanging flyers on doors, making phone calls, sending mailings, running ads at your church, running ads in your neighborhood newsletter, or sending emails.

The faster you consistently get your name out there the faster you change into a dynamic success and you step over the line drawn before you watching your dreams come true.

#8 How to Jump Over a Hurdle When Running Track.

SOMETIMES THINGS DON'T GO AS you expect and you need to recover quickly. Selling real estate is a lot like running track. Running is relatively easy in concept, but running as fast as you can is most challenging. When hurdles are part of the race, danger and risk are added. No matter how good a runner, no one makes it over every hurdle. Accidently misguide your steps and you run right into one. Not lift your foot quite high enough and step into it, causing you to go tumbling as you rack yourself painfully. Track takes discipline, perseverance and a strong desire to get back up and do it again knowing the potential of pain is there every time you approach a hurdle. My coach taught us that the hardest way to get over a hurdle is to slowly walk up and try stepping over it. Hurdles are nearly waist high and if you try getting over 10 hurdles by walking, it's going to take a long time. You'll probably fall over half of them, unable to keep your balance. The best way is to run at them and as you approach, lift one leg straight ahead and simply take a huge running step over it. Nothing on your body will touch the hurdle, and you land in perfect rhythm to approach the next hurdle. It's all about preparation and controlling the timing.

If you run at full speed toward a particular hurdle, and you lift your leg straight ahead of you, but not quite high enough, you step into the top rung knocking it over as you go flying onto the track. How do you react? Does it make you afraid the next time you run toward a hurdle? Does the painful memory of the experience make it not worth trying again?

When I started farming the entire neighborhood where I grew up, it took so many months before I got my first listing that the frustration made me second guess the entire career. I had been running a good race of continuous marketing and self-promotion, but I felt as if I had hit a hurdle so hard with what I spent, that it really wasn't worth it. Most other agents would have already quit, and I was considering the same thing. But I kept going.

I have now listed and/or sold 41 homes just in that area. The income from those houses has paid for my entire marketing expenses … for the next TWENTY years! If you have hit a series of hurdles in your real estate career, and you are considering quitting, brush yourself off and get up again. Don't lie on the pavement wondering if the race is worth it after you hit a hurdle. Analyze what you could do better, learn from the experience, and start running again. Zig Ziglar writes in <u>Ziglar On Selling</u>, "To be the winner you were born to be, you must Plan to Win, Prepare to Win, and Expect to Win."

A few years ago a family called me to come price their house. They lived on my parent's street where I had grown up and where my dad still lived. The husband explained over the phone that he and his wife always had the intention of listing with me, but their nephew was a brand new realtor, and they felt obligated to list their house with him. They had already rented an apartment in a nearby retirement complex, so I agreed to meet with them at the house and gave my pricing opinion even though I knew I wasn't getting the listing. They apologized many times while I was there (since it was clear to all of us they were just using my experience to price the home), and said they really wanted to list with me if it were not for their nephew. I thought highly of them for being so upfront with me. They didn't have to explain the reason they weren't going to be listing with me, but

I certainly appreciated it. We discussed price, and I even gave them suggestions on staging and decluttering. The nephew listed the house for the exact price I suggested and it sold. I got their new address and updated them in my List A just to stay in contact. Since that time they made a point to say the best things about me. In this tough market, their nephew quit real estate and that family has helped me get two other listings.

You may have to learn to forgive a friend who does not use you as their agent. If you've run into this hurdle, it can ram you into the pavement so hard that you struggle to ever recover. Don't hold a grudge, and don't become angry and bitter toward them. I believe you should keep them in your name list to keep sending them mailings. Obviously there is a reason they didn't use you, but it could be they didn't want you to see how much income they have. Maybe they have embarrassing debts. Maybe they had other friends all along they felt they needed to use. Maybe they felt uncomfortable using a family member for buying a house. The fact is if they didn't use you, then you need to get over it immediately. They may be glad to refer you to their friends. It all depends on how you react to these situations if they happen to you.

You might have friends who just bought a house and you're shocked they didn't call you. Don't get mad and say things you can't take back, and don't wallow around trying to analyze what you did wrong. Get back on the running track and jump over other hurdles. If you've just hit a hurdle and you're laying there disgusted and mad, don't just lay there on the pavement for the crowd to watch. Get up, shake it off and start again with the finish line as your ultimate goal of success. Too many agents lose their desire to succeed from past rejection. They lose their focus and they lose their self-confidence. Denis Waitley said, "Goals provide the energy source that powers our lives. One of the best ways we can get the most from the energy we have is to focus it. That is what goals can do for us; concentrate our energy."

DON'T BE THE REASON YOU NEVER FULLY SUCCEED

Sometimes we fail to succeed because of things out of our control, or sometimes we only partially succeed, but we learn to live with it. But many times the thing that keeps us from fully succeeding is ourselves. Why do some agents who have been around a while seem to never sell much? Maybe a buyer visits four open houses, and he ends up picking one agent over all the others as his buyer's agent. What sets some realtors apart from others? Some people have bad habits not healthy for good business. Some people hold on to bad events going on in their lives letting them affect other aspects of their lives negatively. Perhaps an agent is going through a difficult time with a spouse or a child, and that frustration gets channeled into how they conduct business. Sometimes we allow things in our lives which keep us from performing at our best and we wonder why we don't fully succeed.

Last year I had a problem with my right foot. When I wore my black dress shoes, the bottom of my right foot would hurt directly behind my toes. It hurt a little the first day, but the second day my foot already felt bruised as I slipped my foot in the shoe. I started limping a little, and by day three it was extremely sore just pushing down on the accelerator when driving. By the end of the fourth day, my right leg was hurting and even my hips were aching from limping. I started walking slower and going up and down stairs was becoming very painful. By day five, it was clear there was something wrong with me. The pain was so bad I didn't think I could work. I cancelled my showings for that night not thinking I could do that much walking.

The next morning I grabbed my dress shoes, and as I picked them up I heard something in the right shoe. As I reached in there, I felt something. It was a small toy —a plastic ring for our baby to play with. Somehow that little plastic bugger was in my shoe, and I had been sliding my foot in over it – for five days!

How ridiculous to think the negative impact I had allowed it to have. The discomfort was clearly affecting other areas of my life in a bad way. How embarrassing I had not checked inside the shoe. Thank goodness I didn't go to the doctor's office only to find there was a toy in my shoe! It showed me how something so tiny can become such a powerful influence in our lives.

HAVING CLEAR GOALS IN ALL AREAS OF OUR LIVES HELPS US TO FOCUS OUR ACTIONS AND ACHIEVE THOSE GOALS FASTER

When I was in high school it was my privilege to be the Drum Major of the marching band. My senior year we were invited to march in a huge event in downtown Kansas City, The American Royal Parade. It was televised by all the local channels every year. I put on my freshly cleaned white uniform outlined in blue trim, with all its layers including the huge white cape. I shined my 5-foot metal directors staff with a giant silver ball on the end. This huge staff was so ridiculously heavy, it should have been made out of plastic. The band lined up and the drum line started with a loud cadence. Excitement started building, it was our turn to enter into the parade. So there I was, way out in front for all eyes to see in my beautiful uniform, my shiny staff, and my 2-foot tall furry white hat. It even had large yellow tassels matching those on top of the staff. From a distance I looked like a huge Q-Tip. The chin strap to keep the helmet on made it nearly impossible to open my mouth once it was tightened. Now you have the visual, except for my strutting, which is what Drum Majors do while marching. See if you can do this while reading. Stand up, but don't put the book down, now lean all the way back with a 10-pound helmet on so your back is nearly horizontal. Now start walking. As you take each step, kick your legs straight out in front of you so that each leg is as horizontal as your back. That's it, now the other leg, and on and on.

I blew the whistle four times loud and the drum line began its thundering cadence as we advanced forward through downtown Kansas City. Spectators on both sides of the street watched and cheered as the band blasted its way against downtown buildings, echoing everywhere. Of course I couldn't see the crowd very well or even what was ahead of me because I was really into my strutting, leaning all the way back looking up.

This is the perfect time to mention my shoes. They were pure white with slick soles, and I was doing a great job of kicking each leg up with each step as we got closer to the "Live TV Area." I had to make certain the band was playing the featured music so we looked our best on TV. Few bands got invited to march in the American Royal Parade so it was a huge honor, especially knowing everyone I'd ever met would be watching just waiting for our band to come on TV. We wanted to make our community proud. The "Live TV Area" was coming up soon, so it was time for me to start the band playing our best song. I blew my whistle four times and the band revved up. It was show time! The crowd got huge on both sides of the street, and I really began some intense strutting putting that extra effort in leaning way back and really kicking up those legs. Ahead I could see a canopy where the TV Reporters were.

This seems like the best time to mention the American Royal is really about livestock, horses, cattle, etc. And so is the parade. I would guess if a horse has won a major award, it's probably in the parade. We even had some of those award-winning horses right in front of the band. Suddenly I strutted into horse poop, and as one leg went up, so did the other. I landed on my back so hard I blinked out both contacts and threw my shiny staff into the crowd. The breath was knocked out of me to the point I couldn't stand up. My immaculate white uniform had manure (horse diarrhea to be more accurate) all over the cape, my left hip and entire left leg. My huge helmet was hanging off the back of my head choking my neck so I looked like a busted Q-tip with my right shoe missing. Instinctively I wiped the sweat running down my face, but I used the wrong hand and I could smell the manure up my nose. Only a few seconds had passed, but the band was already passing over me trying not to step on me. The drum line was like an incredible machine, and the band was playing better than ever before. It was show time and I had about 10 seconds before reaching the "Live TV Area." So I stood up, and started limping through the band up in front again. Somebody from the crowd, who I couldn't really see through my blurred vision, handed me the staff and said "Yo dude, I hope you're OK. By the way, you're entering the Live TV Area. Man, dude, you smell like S#%&!"

I put my helmet in place, grabbed the staff, tried to stop limping and did the best strutting I could muster. With each kick, the only things I could think of were (1) how much longer to finish the dang "Live TV Area", and (2) how could I scratch off the manure I'd just smeared across my face?

This was one of the most embarrassing moments of my life. But really the only people who saw what took place were those at the front of the band, and the people in the crowd at that exact moment who saw me fall. No one else knew all the details. No one noticed I only had one shoe on or my discolored uniform.

So how did things turn out? The comments I heard were, "The band sounded incredible!" "That's the best they've ever been!" "I'm so proud of what this band has accomplished!" I quickly realized it wasn't about me. From the time I fell during the parade to the time we stopped, I was focused on myself. "What is everyone thinking of me?" "How do I look?" "Am I doing a good job?" "I can't believe I did this?" "Man, I stink!"

I learned a valuable lesson at the American Royal Parade that applies directly to my Real Estate career. With all the marketing to get my name out there, it's really not about me at all. It's all about the client. The client really doesn't care about how many houses I've sold before. They don't care about how I look or what

I drive. They just want their home sold by somebody of integrity who will stay in contact with them and serve their best interests. Serving others with compassion and deeply caring for them is what makes us a success.

#9 OH NO! YOU TOOK TOO MUCH TIME!

IT'S A TOUGH REAL ESTATE MARKET. It just is. With house values down and foreclosures in nearly every neighborhood bringing down values further, most of the houses currently for sale are taking much longer to sell than in the past. It's difficult for many buyers to get loans, and sometimes a house will not even appraise once it is under contract. It's a tough market right now and agents are quitting faster than they're getting in. If it wasn't hard enough to get a listing, it's even harder to get it sold. With numerous listings expiring before they go under contract, many sellers are on the hunt to replace their agent once their listing expires. I have re-listed several houses that expired from other agents in recent months. Yet when my own listings expire, the homeowner almost always extends the listing with *me* for more time. Almost never do I lose a listing to another agent. Why?

I get to know my clients, and I stay in contact with them. We need to build a relationships with them. It's just that simple. Spend time getting to know your clients. I'm amazed how many realtors are proud they can list a house quickly; they have their listing appointments down to 25 minutes. What they've done is become efficient, working fast and telling the client where to sign. But they fail to get to know their clients on a personal level. That may work in a thriving market, but in a tough market it's all about going the extra mile and taking your clients more seriously. My listing appointments typically take around 90 minutes, sometimes longer depending on how much they talk.

We usually spend more time talking about their lives than their house.

Most "people skill" books will encourage you to become a good listener and get your clients to talk about themselves. People love to talk about themselves and their problems, and the more you listen to them talk, the more they will like you for listening. But a friendship will only evolve if you also do a little sharing about yourself too. Tell them some personal details about your life. After listening to them, think of things in your own life they will relate to so you can build trust and a little deeper relationship. Even though people are more interested in their own goals and problems in life more than yours, it can't be a one-sided relationship. Obviously you should let them do most of the talking, but the more ways your clients can bond with you the more likely you are to keep that listing when it comes up for renewal.

A few years ago, I went on a listing appointment where the husband and wife were so reserved and businesslike I couldn't get any personal information from them. They were a closed book with little personality and no humor at all. I knew they were interviewing other agents and wouldn't be signing an agreement that night, but still I could tell from their body language I was not getting this listing. As they showed me around the house I noticed their big screen TV so I told them the following story about one of my open houses.

It was a Sunday in October and I was going to do an open house at a friend's home I had listed. Before I get too far into this, you need to know that it's hard for me to fall asleep. It has always taken me a long time to fall asleep each night, and it's hard for me to wake up in the morning. But once I'm asleep I'm out of it, and if by some horrible event I do wake up everybody is going to pay for it. So there I was having my listing open to the public. I had all the lights on, and my flyers were laid out. I had professional literature about both me and the house. The homeowner baked some cookies and even lit a couple of candles.

I had open house directional pointers at every corner of the neighborhood showing the way. This was the day I expected to sell this home!

Almost every Sunday in October a Kansas City Chiefs football game is on TV, so I had the game on their big screen TV. I had on a white dress shirt and even a tie with footballs all over it. It was a dreary day and nobody had come to the open house yet. Somehow, and let me say this had never happened before in public and shall never ever happen again, I fell asleep. Completely out of it, right there on the couch in front of the TV. My wife tells me I snore loudly sometimes and I'm guessing this might have been one of those days, because all of a sudden I was rudely awakened by a door being slammed shut. I fell off the couch flailing my arms around wondering where I was, coughing and snorting only to find two groups of people standing there looking at the home. Well, really they were looking at *me*. So I patted myself making sure I was dressed, and wiped the drool and tried to figure out what was going on. My first thought was why were all those people in my bedroom, but one of the women immediately started asking questions about the property and I slowly stood up. I had been in such a deep sleep, I still had no idea who I was. As I rubbed my eyes, I realized they were all laughing at me because they had probably been trying to make all kinds of sounds to wake me up. I'm sure I had the imprint of the decorator pillow imbedded on my face.

After sharing this story with the reserved couple on my listing appointment, the wife was laughing out loud as she told a story about a time she fell asleep in college and woke up during the next class. We bonded and I got the listing the next day.

MANY TIMES WE'RE NOT JUST MAKING A SALE, WE'RE MAKING LIFELONG FRIENDS

The better you bond with your clients, the more likely they will extend your listings when they expire. You might not have much reason to call them regularly with so few showings in this tough market, but they should feel that you're *trying* to consistently sell their home. If your sellers think that you've forgotten them or that they always have to call you because they never hear from you anymore, then you might not keep that listing.

Find reasons to stay in contact with them. Perhaps you remember they needed to add mulch to their landscaping this fall and you happen to notice mulch on sale somewhere. They've probably already bought mulch, but a call shows you care and are thinking about them. Emails are also a great way to stay in contact, but I believe they need to hear your voice on a regular basis, even if you're just leaving messages. If you simply cannot think of a reason to keep calling your clients and they've had no showings to follow up with, then call them to see if you can come and retake a few of the inside pictures. That will force a conversation, and you can see your clients face to face.

If you believe you can sell their home, especially with a price reduction, then fight to keep your listing. If you firmly believe that listing needs to be reduced, then make sure you voice your concern and support it with comparable sales. Your sellers want to sell their house, and the last thing you want is for your sellers to relist it with another agent who then gets them to reduce the price.

#10 ONE, TWO, THREE. JUMP!

DID YOU REMEMBER TO STRAP on the parachute? Did you read the safety manual? Did someone show you how and when to pull the rip cord? Did you learn how to land? Or – did you simply jump wondering what the outcome would be?

DID YOU FORGET TO PREPARE?

Skydiving is similar to a career in real estate. Are you prepared? Since you are self employed serving as an independent contractor, you're pretty much on your own to work as hard as you choose. After you pass your real estate exam to get your license, it's up to you as to how many additional classes you take. Which broker do you work for? How much preparation do you need before your first open house? How do you get a personal website? How do you get business cards and For Sale signs? There is a lot to do before your first listing. Many realtors are completely unprepared before they jump out of the plane.

Have you read the entire contract? Have you read it word for word? Can you believe I would ask that? I'm amazed how many real estate agents don't have the slightest idea what they have their clients sign, because they have never read the contract word for word. I don't think they know what it says. When was the last time you read the contract completely, paragraph by paragraph? When I was new I read the contract over and over because I didn't want to screw up. At one of my previous jobs, I was so familiar with the agreements that I could read them upside down to the client as they followed along. That meant I had studied it enough that I pretty much had it memorized. It's concerning how many agents do not understand the inspection process written in the contract, and if the agent is confused then their client probably is too. If you have any questions about the contract, inspections, contingencies, or earnest money, ask your broker exactly what those things mean. Don't have your client sign something you've never read. If your client has a question and you don't know the answer, it's okay to say you don't know and that you'll find out, but in reality you should already know those answers before they ask.

The most time you'll have to learn this information is when you're new. During the first few months when you wish you had business is when you should take advantage of all the classes and training sessions where you can learn. Build a foundation of knowledge in the beginning. The more comfortable you are with explaining the contracts and real estate process to your clients the more confidence you'll have in yourself. I would suggest you role play with other agents in your office. Practice selling them a house and go through the listing papers, page by page. Practice at home by yourself reading the contract out loud. Practice filling out the seller's disclosure on your own house, and practice filling out the seller's estimated proceeds sheet. Look at settlement statements so you are knowledgeable as to what the various fees and expenses are to sell a house.

You may feel overwhelmed. Contracts are long and intimidating, and you may be afraid to estimate your seller's proceeds in fear that you might forget some major fees. You just don't feel confident listing a house yet... maybe not ever. I've seen some of the smartest people get into real estate only to be afraid of the paperwork. They worry about what their friends will say if they ask for a referral. They worry about being rejected if they go on a listing appointment. They're simply afraid of *trying* due to the fear of making mistakes and failing. Norman Vincent Peale wrote in <u>The Power of Positive Thinking</u>, "You do not need to be a victim of worry. Reduced to its simplest form, what is worry? It is simply an unhealthy and destructive mental habit. You were not born with this worry habit. You acquired it. And because you can change any habit and any acquired attitude, you can cast worry from your mind." The Bible says in Isaiah 41:13 "For I am the Lord, your God, who takes hold of your right hand and says to you, Do not fear; I will help you."

To ease fear, go on listing appointments with at least two different agents to see how they explain things. How do they answer questions? How do they handle objections? How do they use their body language and their personalities to make it low stress for the homeowners? At some point, you <u>will</u> be adequately prepared (even if you don't feel confident) and you'll have to do it alone and jump out of the plane.

Don't worry and waste time *over*-preparing. Fear can be a powerful force keeping us from succeeding. Fear is us dwelling on bad things that will likely never happen. Discipline yourself to do the things needed for an appointment and then go do your best. Basically you put on your parachute ...and you jump out of the plane. Whether you need to prospect people by phone calling, following up with potential clients who visited your open house, or spending money you don't have on a mailing that you don't think will work anyway, you need to do it and stay on track. Stay focused and self-disciplined to do something everyday. Near the end of the book, you'll see the importance of being disciplined to do something every single day toward your real estate business. Soon you'll be so busy selling homes, you won't have time to worry about not selling.

#11 The Beautiful Art of Pricing Persuasion.

FOR YOUR PERSONAL PROTECTION, get some body armor and a helmet, and hide them in a sack as you enter your listing appointment. What makes this a tough market right now? One reason is fewer qualified buyers, and those buyers are overly cautious. Wherever you live there are likely too many houses for sale. As a result they are taking longer to sell. Sellers are frustrated and angry, and buyers are looking for deals. In the midst of all this is you trying to make a living. In a tough market, property must be priced correctly or it likely will not sell. A successful realtor will teach their sellers how to appropriately price their homes based on current market conditions.

Some buyers will look at many homes, narrow it down to their top three, but then they wait. They wait for the market to fall more, or they wait for other homes to come on the market beating their top three. Perhaps they expect interest rates to fall, or they simply are overwhelmed with the inventory and don't want to miss out on a better deal they haven't seen yet. Some buyers are just nervous from watching the negativity portrayed in the media and afraid to commit to actually buying. I've typically been more of a listing agent than a buyer's agent. I still work with many buyers, but I just seem to be better at getting listings. A few years ago during the seller's market most all listings would sell fairly quickly. Those listings would lead to even more listings and a variety of buyers, all at the same time. It was a thriving market!

I am fortunate to still list a lot of homes even in this tough market, many of which have expired from previous agents. With it taking longer for homes to sell, many sellers are looking to change listing agents when they expire. Four of the past five years I listed more houses than any other agent in my office. Are you impressed? It sounds wonderful, but of the 21 houses I currently have listed, I have only four under contract as I write this chapter. Last month I took six homes off the market. I would like to stress that none of them got relisted by other agents. One of them is going into foreclosure; two are going to be rented out; the other three are just giving up for a while and are going to try again later. You've heard before, "If You Don't List, You Don't Last." But a new bumper sticker should read, "If You Don't List At Least Two Times The Normal Number Of Homes You Need, You Won't Last." This year I am selling only about half of the homes I have listed, because of the huge inventory of homes for sale. The half that are selling are lower in price than they should be, and sellers are frustrated and angry. Of the half that have not sold this year, sellers are not only frustrated and angry, but also running out of time and patience. I have to say trying to list and sell homes in this tough market is extremely difficult at times. It just is.

…But It's a Great Market for Buyers!

Everything is on sale, interest rates have remained low, and it's a fantastic time for buyers to take advantage of this market. If you are blessed to have listings in this market, you'll need to stress some things from the very beginning when you first meet with your clients. If there is a lot of inventory on the market around their house for sale, your sellers need to know it. They need to see them on paper so they can begin grasping the big picture going on around them. If there are very few homes under contract, and not all that many recent sales, show them the facts. Have it all printed out so they can see this in black and white. They don't want to hear their agent complain or sound hopeless, but your sellers need to know the facts about the kind of market they are up against. If you can let them know how many showings other homes in the area are getting then have that info with you too. The last thing you want is to take on a new listing, and then have no showings for a month with your sellers believing it's all your fault. The more realistic tone you set with them in the beginning will help you during the whole process. It's stressful listing houses in a tough market because many of them will sit and sit and sit with little activity. It's stressful for your clients, because some will take it personally if their house doesn't sell quickly.

MASTER THE ART OF PRICING PERSUASION

When I go on a listing appointment and it's time to discuss the listing price, I show the comps first. We look at days on market of the actives, pendings and solds. We compare what those houses have in size and updates, so they can begin thinking a realistic price. We compare differences in lots. Maybe your sellers have a flat lot backing to a busier road, but all the pendings have finished walkout basements on cul-de-sac lots. When I ask a seller what they think their house is worth right now, it will almost always be worth less than they think. I always let them know my wife and I built our house just five years ago, and I'd hate to think how much less it's worth right now too.

As this conversation unfolds at their kitchen table, I use broad examples of other client's home values so they don't think I'm talking about them directly, and I begin setting the tone for where the conversation needs to go, and then I tell them,

"WHATEVER YOU THINK YOUR HOUSE IS WORTH …IT'S WORTH LESS."

Many times they laugh a nervous laugh, feeling very uncomfortable with the shock of what their house is worth compared to what they were hoping for. No matter how prepared you are with the volumes of paperwork you should have printed out showing them the devalued prices in their area, you must convince them to price their house realistically. This obviously means they won't be getting nearly as much cash in their net proceeds as they were expecting. Many times, your sellers will owe money at closing. At this point, glance around the floor to locate your sack with your body armor in it.

In a seller's market, like we had just a few short years ago, there are fewer listings with numerous buyers. Houses sell faster and closer to asking price. Multiple offers can come in at the same time driving prices higher. Oh, how I miss a seller's market! Now in a buyer's market, there are fewer buyers and a much larger inventory of homes for sale. As a result, sellers get frustrated when their homes take too long to sell and they must reduce their listing prices to compete against the other listings. This forces the other listings to also reduce so they will stay competitive. As houses get low offers and then sell, they become the sold comparables for the next round of listings so values continue falling.

Persuasive Pricing is what this market is all about. You go on a listing appointment with an idea in your head where the house should be priced. In that price range, there happen to be 57 houses for sale in that general area. Of that, only three are currently under contract and only 12 additional homes have sold in the past year. Read through what those houses have that made them sell compared to others still active. Also look at the 57 active listings and see how many of them have already reduced from a higher bracket. Now, drop your price a little and do the same search in the next price category down. How many actives, pendings and solds are in *that* price range? Of those houses how many started off their prices where you were going to price this one? Depending on your city, this can be a rude awakening to both you and your sellers. This is how you do Persuasive Pricing. Give your sellers enough information so *they* will price their home competitively. You cannot price their home for them.

They will definitely ask you where you think it should be priced, so you should have an idea. You say, "Well, Mr. Seller, four years ago I would have priced your home at $285,000, but after looking at these comps I know we'll be less than that. My first thought was listing it for $269,900 in the hopes it would sell for around $265,000, however we have seen that other homes similar to yours are only selling for a maximum of $255,000. There are so many houses for sale right now, it might be tough to get even that much." This will open up a discussion. Mr. and Mrs. Seller will probably look at all the papers you've laid before them, look at each other, and Mrs. Seller will say emphatically, "We'll we paid $268,000 for this home seven years ago and we can't take anything less than that." Ah ha! And now you would love to say, "Mrs. Seller, you must be either deaf or have you not been paying any attention for the last ten minutes? You must be nuts if you seriously think your house is worth anywhere close to $268,000 in this market. If you want to know what I really think, your house probably won't sell for a dime over $245,000!" Wouldn't it be fun to say what we really think? That would be called the art of getting kicked out of their house.

Now is when you need to help them work through all this, using your skilled art of Pricing Persuasion. Typical sellers won't agree with you at first. They firmly believe their house is better than all the others, and for unfortunate reasons all those other houses sold too cheaply. They believe theirs is truly worth more, and you're going to get that higher price for them. They are in complete denial what must take place to price their home to get it sold.

With this first reaction is often a tone of anger, especially if they owe money at closing. They are very clearly fed up with the situation, frustrated with the media, mad at their neighbors who keep reducing, but the only one they can voice this to is you. So for a few minutes you might feel like you're the enemy. They just need to vent, and you're the only one who can listen. When you begin going on numerous listing appointments, this will begin to wear on you. Families are overwhelmed with life, and if you don't plan on going to bed night after night stressing about your job, then you need to reach down and put on your full body armor.

DON'T FORGET THE HELMET - OH MY, IT'S ABOUT TO GET UGLY

At this point, the anxiety will be so great that either Mr. or Mrs. Seller will get up and pace around. They don't know what to do. It's sinking in that everything bad they've see on TV about the housing market has just become their worst nightmare.

Congratulations once again on getting your real estate license. If you thought prospecting and lead generation were hard, here you are now sitting at their kitchen table, sweating with them as they talk about what they're going to do. This is tough to listen to because if their house is overpriced, they're going to lose showings, and probably have little opportunity to get it sold. If they price it a little lower still at a fair price, they could *still* be slightly overpriced with little opportunity to get it sold. Buyers are not looking for a fair price. They want deals – and they want a steal if they can get it. If buyers don't feel like your listing is a "deal," then they'll find a deal in one of the many others for sale instead.

Knowing this, try to put your sellers in the shoes of the buyer and *their* buyer's agent. Explain that if that buyer's agent is going to show them houses on Saturday, how many will they look at? All 57? No, that's too many. Maybe they'll just see 40 of them that day? In reality they'll probably see around five in a day. So the buyer's agent needs to skim through and evaluate 57 houses to narrow it down to the best five. Typically those five will have the most value for the price. They'll have the most updates on the best lots, priced lower than all the others. Either they've been reduced into that price range, or their listing agent helped them price it appropriately from the beginning. Those will be the first homes to sell in that price range in a tough market. Most of the other homes will probably rarely get shown, sitting on the market for months. The sellers begin to realize that if their house has any chance at all of getting a showing, much less selling, it must be priced correctly. Hopefully, they will quickly reduce the price so they don't *follow* other homes already reducing. If you call your sellers and say, "Well, 8 houses dropped their price in the past week, we should really be reducing yours." By then it's probably too late. Had you reduced sooner, you probably would have sold yours before the others had a chance to come down. In a tough market, you have to react before the others and be more aggressive with pricing than the competing houses. While your body armor is still on, secure your helmet, because while you're still at the kitchen table, you will need to bring up the possibility of future price reductions. In a tough market, property must be priced correctly or it likely will not sell. A successful realtor will teach their sellers how to appropriately price their homes based on current market conditions.

A few years ago, after the housing market started changing into a buyer's market, I took a beautiful listing. This gorgeous custom home sat on an amazing wooded lot. We priced this home at $720,000. The sellers were being relocated and moved on to another state. And so here sat their lovely home. During that time, foreclosures were popping up in certain markets due to the sub-prime mess with adjustable ARMS expiring. In the changing economy, thousands of people started getting laid off throughout the country. This high-priced home sat with no showings. It sat and sat and sat. We started reducing the price but really had no idea where to price it, chasing a market that was tanking before our eyes. Over the next 18 months we reduced it several times, eventually down to $550,000. The sellers were frustrated. We had no plan and no forecast model to help. Eventually this exceptional home went under contract for $520,000. During this time, there were 16 other exceptional homes in the same neighborhood for sale but none of them had sold. The appraiser had a most difficult time with no recent sales in the area. He only appraised it for $485,000. Taking too long to react in a falling market can be devastating to selling a house.

WHAT TO DO WHEN VALUES START DROPPING

Some sellers think they'll just wait until the market improves in the spring. This can be smart thinking in a seller's market, but not in a tough buyer's market. If you're now entering a slower season as you take a listing, your sellers need to understand the risk of a falling market. Don't give them false hope that the spring market in six months could be better to sell. That spring market could follow a horribly slow winter market, and the values could drop even more by spring. Yes it might be a busier time, but values could be even lower, as has been the trend in most parts of the country recently. Houses are selling, people are moving, but values are lower in most areas compared to five years ago. There is true danger in chasing a devaluing market. It's very possible that inventories can be even higher in six months going into a busier market, but if few houses sell over the next six months during a slower season, it will probably force the majority of current inventory to continue reducing. Then new listings coming on the market in the spring will have little choice but to continue pricing even more aggressively. The question is: How motivated are your sellers to sell quickly?

Sellers are counting on you for guidance. You need to put on your body armor and be completely honest with them on price. If they believe their house will sell for $350,000 and you know there is no way it can even appraise for more than $320,000, you need to let them know. A good agent will be honest upfront. The last thing you want is to be encouraging a price reduction in three weeks if you didn't suggest it from the beginning. Your sellers will feel betrayed that you think their house is overpriced and you didn't help them price it correctly to begin with. Make certain your sellers understand that no matter what price they reduce to, a buyer will still make a lower offer. They have to be prepared for some negotiation. Remind your sellers that buyers are looking for good deals – a steal if possible.

Don't let your sellers get offended when a low offer comes in. Always negotiate with the goal of finding an acceptable price. They need to be reminded from time to time how many houses they are competing against. Perhaps what was 57 actives is now 63 actives. A few houses that were more expensive have reduced into this price range, and those houses will probably start selling before theirs will. In a tough market it's very unlikely all 63 houses will sell. Some sellers are very motivated and will do what it takes to sell their house. Many times sellers will comment that they hope the loss they are taking on their current house can be recaptured when they buy their next house. Perhaps siblings just inherited their parents' home. If the house is paid for, with no outstanding loans, then they are probably motivated and in a position to price the house correctly to have it sell. Those are great listings, because even if they are reluctant to "give the house away" at least it will sell and your time will be compensated.

#12 Sometimes It's Okay to Not Take a Listing.

LET'S GET BACK TO RUNNING TRACK. You're running hard and fast and you've jumped over the first five hurdles successfully, but as this next hurdle approaches you notice a huge pothole in the track. You have to react quickly to not fall in and ruin your momentum. Other runners fall in, getting trapped in the pothole for a moment, trying to regain composure as they waste time getting their footing again. There will be an occasional listing that you might take because you're so excited to get a listing, but looking back it might be something that you should have stepped over and not agreed to list. Some listings might become potholes which end up draining our time and resources. You can get involved with a seller who absolutely wears you out blaming you for the lack of showings, when all along the house is simply overpriced to the extent it cannot sell. If you find yourself caught up in a listing that is overly exhausting with no hope of ever selling or getting additional business, it will negatively affect the rest of your business and even your personal life. Sometimes it's okay not to take a listing.

I went on a listing appointment earlier this year and I pulled all the comps for the neighborhood and even surrounding areas. I even had with me the total number of properties for sale in the entire zip code with the average days on the market. For the past year the highest sales price in that particular neighborhood was $220,000, and that home was completely updated with new thermal windows, new roof, new furnace, remodeled kitchen and baths, and all new carpet. The house I was sitting in was smaller, only three bedrooms instead of four with none of those updates. There were 18 comparable homes in the area already on the market but only three had sold in the past year with an average price of $204,000. I bet you already have an idea where this subject house should be priced, but heaven forbid the sellers might actually want more money than the market will bear! Has this happened to you?

In this case I explained all the housing data to them and I asked if they had a price in mind. The husband said $250,000. At this point I needed to decide if this listing was worth taking. Can it sell? No. Even if somebody came along and offered $240,000 it simply would not appraise for that much. Sometimes it's OK not to take a listing. I err on the side of taking all the listings I can. From a business standpoint this is not usually a good decision. It can be exhausting resulting in no sales, no extra business, and therefore no income. I did agree to list this home, but after six months it hadn't sold. We only had 8 showings and no offers. They didn't reduce to an acceptable value to get it sold.

There are a couple of reasons that I do take overpriced listings. In the near future the homeowners may become realistic and reduce the price where it should have been priced to begin with. Also, this listing might help you get buyers or additional listings which might actually sell. Maybe this home is on a busy corner and hundreds of people will pass your For Sale sign each day. That's great advertising.

On the other hand, having your sign sit in the yard of a house that doesn't sell month after month reflects on you. People might start thinking, "Don't pick that agent! He's been trying to sell that house for a year and it *still* hasn't sold. There must be something wrong with that agent!" If several months pass with the sellers refusing to reduce to a reasonable price, you might not want to extend the listing when it expires.

What makes a house sell? There are four primary factors:

location, condition, amenities and price. The location can never be changed. Some challenged properties can be tough to sell because of a difficult location. Is the house backing up to a highway or located on a busy corner? I went on a listing appointment where the house had already been on the market for almost two years. They were finishing with their third realtor, and I was about to be the fourth. Directly behind the house had been a vacant lot offering privacy, but now a 24-hour gas station had been built on that vacant lot. Floodlights were on all night and no privacy fence in the world was tall enough. The house had already been reduced by 20% of its value and after 50+ showings, it still had no offers. After meeting with this family for over an hour, I declined the listing and wished them the best as I referred them to another agent in my office. If you feel you are not the best agent to sell a particular home, you do not have to take that listing.

A while back when our middle child, Luke, was 19 months old, he began a phase we affectionately call "mean love." He loved to give kisses and happy smiles, showing all his teeth at the same time. Just adorable, but his teeth were razor-sharp and his fang teeth were dangerous. One day a friend stopped by to let me know he was going to be selling his house and moving out of state, but didn't want to list it with a realtor. He said he would be doing For Sale By Owner (FSBO) but would pay a commission if I had a buyer. Well, it's always pretty insulting when these things happen, but he was nice to actually say it all in person. Luke went over and gave him a big hug when he entered the house. Then Luke followed up with repeated kisses on his thigh as he sat down to tell me the news that he could basically sell his house better than I could. When he mentioned FSBO, Luke's teeth clamped down on my friend's thigh like pliers, biting into his leg as if he learned it from real estate school. You should have heard my friend yell! As I loosened Luke's jaw, we both looked at him as I said "FSBO? Seriously???" Luke must have left a lasting impression, because a few weeks after my friend tried FSBO and didn't get results, I did get the listing. For some reason he is always wearing jeans when he comes over now.

How we react when we first hit a hurdle or fall in a pothole is crucial to how good our outcome can be. There are hundreds of books on overcoming challenges. Countless movies, and some of the most famous passages in the Bible are about this topic. The famous cliché "When life serves you lemons – you make lemonade," is another example of how to positively handle difficult situations. How you react to struggles in your real estate business will mirror your inner strength as you deal with all of life's challenges that come your way.

Three years ago I took a listing on a secluded dead-end street. It had been vacant for three years after the grandmother had passed away. One of the grandsons was a friend so he suggested to his mom that I sell the home. I met his mom at the property. She hadn't been there in a couple of years, and she was appalled to find the backyard had not been mowed in a very long time. Neighbors had been mowing the front, but the back yard had not been moved in a very long time, possibly two years. The grass had grown so tall that it had fallen over and weeds and wild trees were growing up through the dead grass. It's amazing what a privacy fence can hide. The exterior was covered in rotting siding and the side gutter had fallen off lying in the weeds. A car had accidentally hit the support between the garage doors knocking it a few inches off the concrete footing. We couldn't get the front door to unlock, so we waded through the grass and weeds around to the back porch finding the door wide open. Cats and other animals had found shelter in the house and it smelled horrible like mold and animal feces. Vines were growing inside the house through cracks in the storm windows. We quickly looked around the main floor and then headed down the basement stairs finding the finished basement full of standing water. I would guess maybe a foot of standing water, but it had clearly been higher. Standing at the bottom of the stairs, we could see there was so much mold it covered the pool table and sheet-rocked walls. This house was a mess, but it still needed to be sold.

As my friend's mom stood in the kitchen and quickly filled out the seller's disclosure, I began measuring the rooms. I started in the back bedrooms and when I reached down to pick up my tape measure I noticed little tiny black specs on my hand. It must have been dirt from outside so I brushed my hand and kept measuring, thinking nothing of it. The house smelled like a zoo with all the animals that were probably coming back to spend the night in the house. I moved on to the next bedroom finding cat hair all over the carpet. Spiders and insects had taken residence with all the moisture in the basement, and it really needed to be fumigated. While the seller continued filling out the paperwork, I found a clean section of carpet and sat on the living room floor to fill out the sellers' estimated proceeds form. More dirt specs appeared on my hands. Lots of specs. I started feeling itchy, especially inside my dress pants.

Within seconds there were thousands of specs on me. I stood up and ran to Mrs. Seller in the kitchen. I showed her my hands and she stated, "Good grief, you're covered in fleas!"

I unbuttoned my shirt cuff and rolled it up to reveal literally hundreds of thousands of fleas on my arm. She screamed when she looked at her own arms, and we both went running out the back door into the overgrown yard and around to our cars. I could feel fleas in my hair and inside my clothes so I ripped off my shirt thrashing it in the air as I ran. Mrs. Seller was running about the front yard trying to knock them off of her. We were absolutely covered in fleas!

She urgently told me we needed to leave and meet somewhere else later in the week. I got in my SUV and sped home, calling Carrie to tell her what was going on. It took 15 minutes to drive home and I could feel them biting me all over. They covered my face and I watched them jump from my hands as I drove. I pulled in the garage so fast I almost rammed the house. I stripped down, laying all my clothes and shoes on the garage floor and set off foggers, hoping they would all stay in the garage and die fast. I raced upstairs to the bathroom and took enough showers until I figured they must have all gone down the drain. Over the next few hours, hundreds of bites appeared on me, covering my legs. I have never itched so badly in my life.

After they professionally fumigated the house and yard, I listed the house. I went there many times showing it to investors, but the house never sold. Sometimes it's okay to not take a listing.

#13   STAGING CAN BE A VERY SENSITIVE TOPIC.

WHEN I MEET A SELLER for the first time and they show me their home, I often give them a list of things they should change before I come back to list it. Maybe they just need to de-clutter some rooms so they show better. Sometimes they need to take pictures down and repaint some walls, or perhaps their landscaping needs cleaning up. The condition and price are usually the only things the homeowner can change, although sometimes amenities can also be added with finishing a basement, creating a room addition, or building a new custom deck. All agents should help their customers with staging. Sometimes, if their budget allows, it's good to refer sellers to a real staging company. Most of my clients don't want to pay for that, but I usually suggest it. If you feel a room is too crowded and the house would show better with certain pieces of furniture removed, offer the idea. Cleaning off the front of the refrigerator helps greatly, but sometimes the sellers need to remove half the things on their kitchen counter too. Maybe they need a new kitchen rug because they haven't noticed a large hole is wearing through it. Doing these small things can be significant in helping a house sell faster. The difficulty comes with how to offer suggestions.

HOW TO STRAIN A GOOD FRIENDSHIP

Many times it's easier to offer suggestions on how to improve the condition of a house if the sellers are strangers. But if these are friends and you think you're going to start suggesting they clean their kitchen or put away personal things, then you're about to venture into the "forbidden zone" where friends don't go and you will unintentionally offend them. I sold some friends a house a few years ago. Three years later he got transferred and they called me to sell it for them. During those three years they had two kids, and she was pregnant with the third. You should have seen the mess! Clutter was everywhere. It showed much worse than I expected, especially considering they knew I was coming over. I could tell Mrs. Seller was already irritable with their kids and the stress of moving to a different city. After we had filled out all the listing papers, Mr. Seller asked if they should do anything to the house to help it show better. Can you believe he said it out loud? He was probably hoping I would say all the things he felt like he couldn't tell his wife. By the time I was finished, he also had his share of assignments. The kitchen counters were covered in baby bottles, opened boxes of cereal on their sides, and numerous other things like tools that really belonged in the garage. My friend had his golf bags and shoes in the entry way, and they had enough baby pictures hanging on all the walls for a family of 50. Baby swings, stacks of magazines, a pile of DVD's their oldest kept getting out by the couch, and Toys! Toys! Toys! Mrs. Seller must have been scrapbooking because she reluctantly pushed all that to the other end of the dining room table. No way was this house ready to be shown, much less to even begin taking pictures. We joked around about ways they could keep the house a little cleaner for showings, and I even suggested they rearrange some furniture, which we did while I was there. But when I suggested they take down this huge needlepoint doily thing hanging in the living room, Mrs. Seller went ballistic. Her grandma had made it and there was no way that was coming down, and how insulting for me to suggest it!

At that point Mrs. Seller began loudly listing every reason why she didn't want to move, using a variety of hand gestures to make each point clear. It was worthy of a David Letterman's Top 10 List for not wanting to move. It began with leaving all their friends behind, and concluded that the house couldn't sell anyway with Mr. Seller's tools in the kitchen and "golfing crap" in the entry. I remember backing into the corner around her fourth point, sitting in a chair as far away as possible. So what happened?

They did all the things I asked before the broker tour the following week. It was impressive and showed like a completely different home on the inside. Mrs. Seller was even able to keep the house looking great for all the showings until it went under contract. It's difficult to offer suggestions to other people, especially when it's about how they live. Everyone wants to look their best at all times, and to have somebody analyze how they live, room by room, can be taken poorly by many people. Nobody likes to be criticized, so how we handle these "staging" conversations is crucial to having them improve the condition.

THE BETTER A PROPERTY SHOWS, THE FASTER IT WILL SELL

Staging a home isn't just moving the couch and setting up some candles around a new picture frame; it's more than rearranging the items in a bookcase. Staging involves everything that can be done to make a house more saleable. It can involve pruning bushes all around the house, planting some flowers out front, washing the front door, or repainting a couple of interior rooms that are currently bright purple to something neutral. Staging can also involve putting away the litter box, and maybe adding a Glade Plug-In.

My brother and I sold my parents' house last year. Their neighborhood had been struggling with values in this tough market, which I well knew since I had been the primary listing agent in the area for the past few years. There hadn't been many improvements made to the house in the past 25 years. My mom loved to wallpaper. In fact, every single room in the house was wallpapered! The entire entry and hallway had three layers as was the trend thirty years ago. Someday the trend will probably return, but for right now – wallpaper is out. My brother and I considered renting and then selling it in the future in a better market, but since this was the home where we grew up, I just didn't want strangers sleeping in my old bedroom while we tried to collect rent, wondering if they were trashing our house. Furthermore, if we planned on making it a rental, we'd still need to remodel it. Even if we were to sell it as-is we would probably have needed to fix some things anyway to satisfy an FHA appraisal. So we fixed a crack in the foundation where water seeped in, and had the front stoop and concrete steps repoured where they had settled.

Then the big question came into play. How much more remodeling should we do? At what point would we spend too much money that we'd never get it back? The house was so dated that we decided it would be in our best interest to do some remodeling or it might not even sell at all. With numerous other homes already on the market in the neighborhood, we hired handymen and painters to help speed things up. We started with the kitchen: New floor, countertops, sink and backsplash, light fixtures and all new appliances. Then a new roof. We had an older composition roof torn off that was over a wooden shake roof, so this was expensive. We had all the wallpaper removed and then painted a neutral beige throughout. After doing minimal remodeling in the bathrooms, we had the entire house re-carpeted. The basement wall was professionally sealed where it was cracked, and then we had the basement refinished, adding new carpet. Two damaged windows needed to be replaced. The exterior needed to be repainted, and we changed every single light fixture to give a new look. We spent approximately $35,000 on remodeling. Then we had the large trees trimmed and redid most of the landscaping. There was much more we could have done, but we needed a stopping point. The bathrooms, still dated, were simply not part of the budget.

I wish I had used a realtor who was good at the art of Pricing Persuasion to advise me, because I listed the house too high at $159,900. Four years ago I could have easily sold this house in the $150's, but not in this market. I looked at the comparable sales, and I should have known better. This, however, was the home I grew up in. Most of my childhood memories were from that house. I became a typical seller. Not only was this house better than all the others, I just knew buyers would jump at it. We listed it just as we entered the busy spring market, but had only one showing in three weeks. We reduced it to $149,900, but after a couple more weeks at that price, we had no showings. There were no other sales in the neighborhood either, and houses were coming down in price. After my brother and I reduced it to $145,000 the showings started, but the comments were: no fence, bathrooms still dated, but the rest of the house was fantastic. No offers and a couple of other lower-priced homes in the neighborhood sold instead.

More time passed and we reduced to $137,500. My brother was a realistic seller who was ready to reduce more to unload it. By now we were nearing the end of the spring market, and many more houses had come on the market. A foreclosure directly across the street that had been listed for $85,000, was already reduced to $74,900. We reduced again to $133,500. At that point, I had no intention of reducing any more. I was mad at the media for saying how bad the market was and scaring buyers. I was mad at the foreclosures driving down values. I was mad we had spent so much money on the house. We were now looking at netting below $100,000 after the improvements, the buyer's agent's commission, and closing costs. And I was mostly mad we still didn't have it sold. The house looked great, in fact much better than when we were growing up there. My parents would have loved to see how great it looked. Mom never did like that dated green kitchen even when it was in style.

We had transformed that house into something we were proud of, but it wasn't selling for what we expected. A few weeks later we got an offer for $114,000. I was not a happy seller and I would have become a listing agent's worst nightmare. How insulting to get an offer like that! No way would we even consider thinking about a counter offer. My first thought was to take a big black marker and write "REJECTED" across the first page and fax back.

My brother suggested we counter back, and so we did many times back and forth. We arrived at a price, and then their inspector found major cracks inside the chimney. The fireplace hadn't been used in at least 15 years, so it didn't occur to us that it might have deteriorated inside. By the time we renegotiated on that issue, we had sold the house for right at $120,000. Looking back, we could have sold it as-is and probably netted more money.

I NOW UNDERSTOOD EXACTLY HOW BAD IT WAS TO SELL A HOUSE IN A TOUGH MARKET

I currently have a house listed that has been on the market for about four months. We've reduced it a couple of times, but the feedback from showings continues to say that the kitchen is "just too dated." The homeowner is having new countertops put in this week and new appliances. It will only cost approximately $2300 to do that through a friend of her family. Money well spent because the cabinets look great and the floor is already fairly new. This small investment will likely sell the house.

If your sellers need to invest a few thousand dollars to improve the condition, they might or might not get that money back. Just because they repaint and recarpet the entire house doesn't mean you can raise the price by that same amount in this market. Sometimes these improvements are necessary just to get a home to sell. Yes, they should get their home looking as good as possible. Yes, they should do whatever they can to help it sell faster with updates and staging …but in a tough market they might or might not get all their money back.

#14 Make Sure You Ask These Questions Before You Take a Listing.

MANY PEOPLE HAVE BEEN LAID off work over the past few years and the foreclosure rate is so high that we're *all* feeling the negative effects. When you go on a listing appointment, you must estimate your sellers' proceeds so they know how much money they should be netting. This information is as much about financial warning signs as it is about estimating their proceeds. What you are looking for are accurate loan balances. Many times sellers don't just have one loan, but may also have other lines of credit tied to the house. Unfortunately, many times sellers don't realize they owe more on the house than it's worth in the current housing market. You need to know if they are going to have to bring thousands of dollars to closing in order to sell their home.

I had a house listed for sale, and my clients told me they had missed a payment. They weren't completely honest with me, because they were actually five months behind on their mortgage. They also had a home equity line of credit tied to the house they didn't mention. They moved out a week after I listed it without telling me, and I got a call one morning from a man who had bought the house at auction on the courthouse steps. He was at the house changing the locks and told me to come get my sign and lockbox. Wow! I had no idea the house was going up for auction and the owners were too embarrassed to tell me they had been foreclosed on. I had just wasted a lot of time and effort marketing a house that my sellers couldn't sell.

Don't be afraid to ask questions. Hopefully your sellers are not too embarrassed to be completely honest about their financial situation. If a family is downsizing because the husband lost his job, ask how many months they can make payments before they run out of money. If they have started missing payments, ask if they have their lenders' permission to do a short sale.

About a year ago I got a call to potentially list a house that had already been on the market for ten months. In my opinion it was still overpriced even though they had reduced it twice during the year. I was not very excited about getting this listing. I had another listing three blocks away and I knew these sellers were interviewing different agents in the area to relist it. I went prepared. I took the Comparative Market Analysis showing where their home needed to be priced (which was even lower than their current reduced price), loaded up my sign, lockbox, listing packet, calculator, etc., just in case they should choose me.

Well, right before I left, my daughter Lydia had a dirty diaper, *really dirty* – one of those requiring both my wife and me to change. Lydia's rear end was pretty red, so we had to use some *Boudreaux's Butt Paste* on her redness. It's greasy, yet soothing, and probably feels good on a diaper rash. Lydia was thrashing around during the diaper changing and got butt paste all over my dress pants and even some on my glasses. I quickly changed pants, and raced to the listing appointment. I arrived a little early, and after introducing myself to these complete strangers, I shook their hands. I remembered their names and made a little small talk and then I began my listing presentation. I estimated their proceeds to their surprise, because their previous listing agent had apparently never done so. Neither had any of the other agents they were interviewing that week. I quickly realized they owned more on their loan than the house would sell for. They made it clear they had no cash to bring to closing so I was getting even less enthusiastic about listing this home. It was clear they would not be able to reduce the price anymore. In fact they already owed money at closing with their current list price which they were not pleased to find out.

I noticed they kept looking at my hair, and after a while it annoyed me that they weren't paying attention to my presentation. I reached up touching my glasses and felt goo. Ah yes, I had Butt Paste in my hair. With three children, ages four and under, our normal topics of conversation have become most fascinating to our friends. "Breast feeding," "baby puke," and the ever so popular "Butt Paste" have become the norm for us to discuss.

So I announced to these potential sellers, "Oh no, I have Butt Paste in my hair." They didn't look at all pleased with this discovery especially since I had just made them mad by stating their home was at least $20,000 overpriced and they already owed money they didn't have. Now they realized they had just shaken hands with a man who apparently had a serious personal problem.

I could tell they had no intention of reducing their price, and I clearly wasn't getting the listing anyway, so I didn't think they needed to know I had 3 little kids. In fact I didn't think they needed much of an explanation about the Butt Paste. I simply informed them that normally when I use Butt Paste I'm careful not to get it on my hands much less in my hair, but this time I made such a mess with it I even had to change my pants right before coming over. Mrs. Potential Seller's mouth dropped open slightly, with the most horrific look of disgust I'd ever seen. At that point there really wasn't much left to say in my presentation, so I rubbed the butt paste through my hair a little more and told them I had another appointment to get to. There was no shaking hands at the end as they ushered me quickly to the door. No, I did not get that listing, but I did do a very nice presentation.

HAVING SOFT HANDS MIGHT NOT BE ENOUGH

Having three kids all very close in age has impacted my career in a most challenging way. I was getting a listing presentation put together and printing it out right before I needed to leave. My wife had just left for the grocery store with our four year old, Lydia. Before she headed out the door she put Luke (21 months old) in his crib for a nap. I was in my office frantically getting my papers together. I had just put on my dress clothes and was about to print the client's CMA when I thought I heard noises from upstairs. I assumed that Luke was still asleep in his crib, so I continued working. After another few minutes I heard more noises, this time coming from the other end of the house. Still rushing, I ignored it and kept working. But when I figured out the noises were coming from our master bedroom, I rushed upstairs.

This was the day Luke discovered he could get out of his crib. He was inside the shower in the master bathroom squirting hair conditioner all over himself and all over the floor of the shower. I've never seen a little boy having so much fun sliding around. There was no possible way he could stand up. He had squirted a 3-year supply of hair conditioner all over everything! As I grabbed him in my dress clothes, he slipped out of my hands. I realized I was in trouble, because Carrie had just spent all morning cleaning the entire house for friends to come over that night. I took off my dress clothes and stripped him down to his diaper. I rushed him back to his crib and shut his door. Then I took a shower trying to wash away all this conditioner before Carrie got home. Do you know how hard it is to stand up with that much slippery conditioner?! After I frantically got it all washed down the drain, I got dressed again and as I rushed downstairs, I saw Luke. He had gotten out of his crib again, made it downstairs and into the pantry. He was shaking a mega-sized box of Cheez-Its upside down everywhere! So I started sweeping up Cheez-Its into piles, barely noticing a few hundred had gone down the floor vent by the pantry. There just wasn't time to get them out when in walked Carrie and Lydia. I ended up making it to my listing appointment about 45 minutes late, explaining what had happened as I drove to the appointment. As I shook their hands upon arrival, Mrs. Seller said, "What incredibly soft hands you have!" I was still pretty frazzled when I arrived after speeding there as fast as possible. I didn't know what to say, so I stated I used conditioner on my hands. The husband didn't seem impressed. I don't think the wife had filled him in on the reason why I was so late. To make things worse, because of the conditioner/Cheeze-It fiasco, I didn't have my listing presentation printed. I did not get the listing. On the positive side however, when our furnace came on that night it filled the downstairs with a nice toasty aroma of Cheez-Its from that floor vent

#15 Keep It Clean.

I'M A SLOB. There I said it out loud. I'm messy, and I don't like the paperwork in this business, so I usually have stacks of it needing to be filed. I leave dirty clothes on the floor, I don't rinse out my dishes, and I sometimes leave the toilet seat up. It drives my wife crazy!

How embarrassing if you should see the inside of my Toyota 4-Runner! The outside is usually very clean because my name, phone number, website, and company info are printed on the glass, but what a mess inside. I try to keep it clean, but how it continues to be a mess I just don't understand. If you never have clients in your car, then you can keep it as trashed as you please, but if people are riding around with you, it needs to be immaculate. Keep it vacuumed and smelling good. Remove signs from the back so clients don't hear them banging around. For me this is a constant challenge.

Even more important is our appearance. We can be slobs at home, but out in public we have to look our best. I'm not saying we have to wear suits while working, but we should all have clean hands and fingernails, especially if we are going over paperwork and pointing where clients need to sign. Having brushed teeth, good breath, clean shoes, and combed hair are all important. If you are coming into this business with long hair or a bushy beard and you're wondering if you need a hair cut then ask your broker or other agents for advice. Examine your personal appearance from time to time. Nose hair and ear hair are not in style and easy to remove if need be. If you have body piercings on your face then it might be wise to examine what your clientele will be most comfortable with. How easily clients relate to us helps determine our success.

I received a call from a couple wanting me to show them some homes the next morning. I knew my SUV was a mess with lots of files in both the front and back seats and a variety of fast food containers scattered here and there. Two baby seats were strapped in the backseat. Do you know how hard it is to get those car seats strapped in tightly? It takes all day to get the things installed, and sometimes it's even harder to get them back out. Late the night before after all our kids were in bed, I cleaned all the trash out and began to get it cleaned for my appointment. I removed the easiest car seat, leaving the other one in place. That way the husband could sit in the front and his wife would still have room in the back. I didn't think she would mind.

The next morning I realized I had not removed the files, so I just stacked them all up and laid them in the remaining car seat. (I quite often use it as an inbox while driving around). Halloween was the following week, and my wife had just bought our kids some fake plastic bugs and spiders. Apparently there have been great advancements in the making of plastic spiders and creepy bugs because these looked lifelike – much more realistic than I'd remembered them from years ago. I didn't have time to take them back in the house, so I laid the bag in the baby's car seat, and headed to the couple's house to pick them up.

I selected five homes to show, and as we drove towards the last home, I realized I had missed my turn. I told everyone to hang on as I made a sharp U-turn, causing the car seat to tip just enough that the files dumped over onto Mrs. Buyer. Unfortunately, her hands were busy grabbing the files when the bag of bugs and spiders emptied onto her lap. I can still hear her frantic screaming! She panicked, throwing them everywhere! She spastically freaked out until she got all of them off of her.

After finally throwing most of the spiders out the window, she smacked me on the back of my head with the files. Mr. Buyer was laughing so hard in the front seat he could barely even talk, infuriating Mrs. Buyer to no end. He finally said through his laughter that was only the second time in his life that he had heard his wife cuss. Since then, I've made sure that my SUV is completely cleaned out for clients.

Another couple was referred to me to show them some houses. Having been permanent missionaries in Africa for 30 years, they had just retired from the mission field. They were moving back to the United States and wanted to live in Kansas City to be close to their kids who were now grown with kids of their own. Even though I'm a deacon and very involved at a local Baptist Church, I was in no way feeling in the same league as a couple who had lived as foreign missionaries. I was a bit intimidated knowing these people were probably "perfect Christians." Usually I joke around with clients, but I didn't know what would be appropriate so I tried to keep things very professional.

I wanted to showcase the city since this couple really didn't know anything about Kansas City or the suburbs. I bought a map of the city, bottles of water, and made sure I had gum and breath mints. I even washed my SUV and vacuumed the inside. I cleaned the wheels by hand and also detailed the inside. Knowing cleanliness is next to Godliness, I also polished my shoes and made sure to dress up more than usual. I'm not easily intimidated, but in this case I really wanted to make them happy and go the extra mile.

One day when we were looking at houses, Mrs. Buyer asked if I had any Tylenol. She had been to the doctor that morning before we went looking at homes. This was one of those days that involved a lot of driving to get to another part of the city, and I could tell she wasn't at her best. They explained that because of their rural isolation in Africa, that they rarely got to see a doctor. When we finished looking at houses I dropped them off and I went home. A few minutes later I got a call from Mr. Buyer. He asked in the most serious tone, "Could you check and see if my wife left something in your back seat?" On my way out to the garage to check, I asked what I should be looking for. Was it a scarf or maybe an umbrella?

Before he could answer, I had opened the back door and there was the missing object – Mrs. Buyer's bra! "Yes I found it, and I'm holding it right now. How in the world did your wife's bra get in my backseat???"

I could hear the embarrassment in Mr. Buyer's voice after learning that it was really there. He told his wife in the background, "Yes dear, he found it. He's holding it right now." He then explained that Mrs. Buyer had her very first mammogram that morning which caused the discomfort and was the reason she was asking for Tylenol. After we had left the last house she had taken off her bra to be more comfortable. She hid it in her in her purse thinking no one would know, but unfortunately it fell out in my back seat! I started laughing, and then he started laughing. It was wonderful knowing they weren't perfect after all. I let him know I would be glad to put their names on it and drop it in the offering plate at church on Sunday so it could get back to them. It was great joking around with them.

#16 DON'T GET DEPRESSED WHEN THINGS DON'T GO AS YOU WOULD LIKE.

DEPRESSION IS THE NUMBER ONE REASON why there is such a high turnover rate in sales. People get frustrated with their lack of success; that frustration quickly leads to disappointment in how they see themselves. Then depression sets in and they are done for. By then it's nearly impossible for a depressed sales person to sell much of anything. They quit or get fired for poor performance on the job. What has gone wrong? Unfortunately, I can easily tell you.

I entered real estate after having been successful in my other jobs and sales positions. Even though I never really enjoyed any of my previous jobs, I always worked hard enough at them to succeed. I firmly believed I would quickly become a rapid success as a realtor and show everyone else how it's done. Not only did that not happen, but I was selling nothing for months and months. In my eyes I was a public failure at my new career.

DON'T COMPARE YOUR WEAKEST POINTS TO OTHERS' GREATEST STRENGTHS

What did I do? I made it worse. I looked at the successful agents in my office who were consistently selling and I compared myself to them. It's like being overweight and joining a fitness center to work out. You're on a plan to get from point A to point B, but after working out consistently four times a week and not seeing any immediate results you get a little frustrated. Weeks pass and you see all these other beautiful people in prime condition working out, running on treadmills, looking how we always wanted to look. They start to look sickeningly perfect, and after a while it starts to eat at us and we think how unfair life is. It's easy to compare what we are lacking in to their strengths. Then we get frustrated and disgusted. This quickly becomes a destructive habit and it will place you in a no win position. I know why one of the Ten Commandments in the Bible says "Do Not Covet." All of a sudden I found myself struggling with jealousy because I wanted to be as successful as these other agents and it just wasn't happening for me. I was so depressed I didn't even want to go to the office and be reminded of how bad I was doing. I felt inferior and it started having an impact on all other areas of my life. I would share my frustration with my family. My dad, who only wanted the very best for my life, would quickly offer his free advice – "You're wasting your life! You're spending all your savings on mailings and gas! Cut your losses and get your resume out there! Go get a real job with benefits!"

So what happened? A broker even suggested I quit after completing my first full year in 1998. I had failed that year, but I didn't quit. I developed a clear to-do list, which became my new action plan, on how to get from point A to point B. I developed an attitude that I would become successful real estate agent or I would die trying. I started selling a few more houses during my 3rd year, and my sales started to really climb in my 4th and 5th years. I was making money selling houses! In fact, I was making a lot of money. I was making more money than all my friends who had told me to quit. I got married during my 5th year and by the end of my 6th and 7th years I was selling more than I ever really expected. We moved to a new home and had our first baby in 2006, at the peak of the real estate market in the Midwest. Then times quickly changed.

Since That Time We Have Entered a Very Tough Market to Sell Houses

I decided to work harder as the market shifted, and even with the difficult economy my sales ranked me as the Top Selling Realtor in my office for 2008. <u>I was the #1 Top selling agent</u>! That was the year our 2nd baby was born, and sadly my dad passed away 3 months later. I was glad he got to see how successful I was. Dad had come over to our house every day to hang out since we lived close by. He always asked about each client and how things were going on every transaction, wanting me to get even more business. He loved to see the commission checks since he had helped me get numerous listings in his neighborhood and from his friends. I still remember when I saved four commission checks to show him at the same time. That day he stated, "Aren't you glad you stuck with it?" as if the whole thing was his idea! I knew he was proud of me.

Maybe you are a brand new Realtor. You only got your real estate license because you were laid off from your old job. Because nobody else was hiring, you got into real estate as a last resort. Now everyone is telling you to get out of real estate because your timing is horrible, and you should just send your resume everywhere else instead.

Your Timing May Be Better Than They Think

They would be correct in saying even most successful realtors are making less money than they used to – but not all. What will possibly happen over the next few years is more realtors will quit than will continue. We will also see several agents sign up but not last very long since they won't know what it takes to succeed. Many of the part-time realtors who used to sell enough houses to pay their bills will be faced with a situation where they no longer sell enough to break even. We'll possibly even see some Title Companies close their doors. Many small mortgage companies have already shut down. As these trends continue, the companies that ride through these difficult times will emerge on the other side with fewer competitors. When we re-enter a good market, a seller's market, there will be fewer realtors to participate. Once again we'll see lots of new people getting their real estate licenses, but they won't be able to compete with the established realtors who are now prospecting and building name recognition.

THE TIME IS NOW TO BUILD A FOUNDATION TO THRIVE WITH

Agents who are putting in the hard work now will literally thrive when the market picks up again. The agents starting out now will have the opportunity to lay a powerful foundation that will catapult them to levels of success that other realtors will completely miss. If you treat this business seriously and invest your time and money into marketing yourself to create name recognition, you will reap great rewards in the near future. If you do some consistent prospecting and lead generation for many months in a row, you will begin creating a loyalty among your COI list that will drive a multitude of referrals your way. Concentrate on developing relationships, work on your skills of listening to your clients, and figure out what you can do for them. If you can master the art of pricing, conduct effective open houses, and communicate well with your clients, you will find yourself quickly making money in this housing market.

THE BEST TIME TO GET IN REAL ESTATE IS RIGHT NOW

Don't get depressed looking at the market today. Thomas Edison once said, "Opportunity is missed by most people because it is dressed in overalls and looks like work."

#17 EEEEW! PLEASE TELL ME THAT WASN'T CONTAGIOUS!?

THREE YEARS AGO I SHOWED a home that impacted my personal life. I had shown some homes to a family of just total clean freaks. Mrs. Buyer paid so much attention to neatness that if she tracked a leaf or blade of grass into my car, she made sure to throw it back out. She commented on each house's cleanliness or lack thereof. I showed them this one particular home on a cold December day. During the weeks leading up to this day Mrs. Buyer had been encouraging me to get a flu shot because we had a new baby at home. Ironically, she made sure to remind me again that day also and stressed how important it was to wash our hands on a regular basis. Let's just go ahead and call her a "germophobe".

We arrived at the 4th house, I rang the doorbell and no one answered. I opened the door and yelled hello as I always do upon entering. We had looked around the entire main floor and headed upstairs. After viewing the smaller bedrooms, we entered the master bedroom. Just as we all went in, we heard a woman whispering from the bed with a raspy sick-sounding voice. "Hi, I'm sorry to be here. I came home sick from work." This woman was a raging epidemic!

That was all Mrs. Buyer needed to vacate the house immediately. As we all ran out the door, I realized I had touched every doorknob in the house. I tried hard not to touch my lips or pick my nose as I thought about the billions of germs on our hands. Mrs. Buyer was a panic-stricken mess as I started the engine. She tried not to breathe in and suggested we go somewhere immediately to wash our hands. Unfortunately, we all did get sick, and a few days later my entire family was down and out too. From this I learned to carry hand-sanitizer in the console of all our vehicles. Now, when a client leaves a house commenting on the filth, I can now say "I have these wipes just for this kind of occasion." It puts everyone at ease and makes me look like the thoughtful hero.

Negativity is a sickness that also spreads like stomach flu. Once somebody has it, it spreads quickly incapacitating its victims. The next few suggestions all go hand-in hand. If you struggle with these as I still do, it could be easy to slip into a self-defeated attitude and never achieve all that you should be.

IGNORE THE ADVICE OF NEGATIVE PEOPLE

Even though they mean well, negative people don't share your vision and passion, and a negative influence is definitely contagious. I had a college roommate whose mom would visit, and she loved to talk and talk and talk. She was really entertaining to listen to, full of information on everyone she knew. However my roommate was always embarrassed when she'd come into our dorm room, because she had so much tell us. She had this saying, "Now I'm not one to repeat gossip, so ya'll gonna have to listen up the first time." And then she'd tell her son what she had heard about all his high school friends. He would then correct her on negative misinformation before she spread it to other people.

Negative influences are easy to spread, but fortunately positive ones are too. For this exact reason, we should associate ourselves with positive and encouraging people. You've heard that "success breeds success." Well negativity breeds negativity, which is why having the wrong friends applying bad peer pressure in high school and college can lead to poor decision making. If you spend a lot of time watching news channels on TV where they continuously report the bad side of the economy and housing market, you'll wear down. Obviously it's a tough market to sell houses, hence the title of the book. But many hard working realtors are selling homes and enjoying a wonderful lifestyle. Flood your mind with all the wonderful opportunities this market is creating for you. Read encouraging books to develop your selling skills. Smile, and show genuine interest in other people when you talk with them. The more positive your attitude, the more people will be attracted to you.

#18 You Must Have the Support of Your Family

ONE OF THE MOST DIFFICULT things for me when I got my real estate license was having a parent or friend criticize me for being in sales and self employed – especially as a realtor. My dad valued the security of being an employee where one has a clear job to do and just has to show up, get the job done, and receive a consistent paycheck every two weeks. "With benefits," he would add. My dad saw jobs as safe and the rewards consistent. I, however, craved the opportunity to make as much money as possible while enjoying a flexible schedule that changed each day. My dad had been a Marine but spent most of his career as an elementary school principal. My mom, on the other hand, was an elementary school teacher with a personality very different from my dad. She enjoyed taking more risks in life and encouraged changing things up a bit. She would have appreciated the advantages of my being a full-time realtor. She passed away a few months after I got my license, so she didn't get to see me sell my first house.

A spouse greatly affects your attitude and success. If you plan on being successful in real estate and you don't have complete support from your spouse, either your career or your marriage will fail. You cannot associate with negative people on a daily basis and expect to succeed. If your spouse is your biggest fan, you will have both a successful career and an exceptional marriage. Your spouse must support your constantly changing schedule; they must support you without complaining. The reaction of your spouse and kids to the demands placed on your schedule will either give you confidence and reassurance or it will create conflicts. Either they will respect and appreciate your schedule, or they'll become bitter and resentful of it. My family knows that no matter what I'm doing, I may get interrupted for business while watching TV, mowing the yard, working out, taking our kids to swim, eating at a restaurant, or going to a baseball game. If we started eating dinner at home and my cell phone rings, I quite often answer it. Sometimes I put the call into voicemail, but I always call them back immediately. If we're out shopping, then I almost always answer it. I don't like shopping anyway. These calls don't usually take very long, and every single call is important. It's how I choose to conduct my business.

Some agents rudely announce on their voicemail that they only return calls during certain limited hours of the day, and don't return any calls at night. I think those agents are in the wrong business and doing their clients a disservice by not being available. One thing has become very clear to me over the last few years of observing that behavior in certain other agents – I sell more than they do. Don't you just look forward to the day when you sell more than the agents you compare yourself to? If you follow the successful tips in this book, then your success as a realtor is just around the corner. You'll even find you are home more than anyone who has a regular job. If my wife needs me to be home so she can go run errands, I can schedule it so I'm home. We're actually home most of the time together, and we never seem to get sick of each other!

My wife is not a realtor; she raises our children, listens to all my frustrations and funny stories from selling houses, but she has no desire to drive people around all day and not have them buy anything. During the busy season, you might need to schedule in some family time, but for the most part you'll be home much more than you think. Compare this job to somebody in full-time sales who has to travel each week, leaving for the airport early Monday morning and not flying back home until Friday afternoon. Their weekend is spent getting ready to leave town again, cleaning clothes and repacking bags. You'll find a very busy full-time realtor is still home much of the time. Realtors might work 40-plus hours a week, but it's chopped up all over the day. We simply work a unique schedule with flexibility as the key.

Working from home, while having little kids, has created some unique challenges and experiences that I would never have experienced at a regular 9 to 5 job. Our four-year old daughter, Lydia, never learned to open the exterior doors of the house, and therefore never learned that she could escape. But our two-year old son, Luke, learned this quickly. He can open any door and enjoys going into the garage and outside. For this reason we are not encouraging our baby, Caleb, to learn to walk. After we realized Luke could do this we installed locks on the inside of all the exterior doors near the top of each door. Now he can't leave, and we can't get in. When my wife or I come home we must call in advance so a door can be unlocked at the top. The fun and frustration is that Luke can also lock the door handles, so we've learned the hard way to have extra sets of keys to let ourselves back in.

Recently my wife and Lydia were out on the deck. I was about to leave for an appointment, and had just stepped out on the deck to say goodbye. As soon as I did, I heard Luke lock the door from inside. So there we were out on the deck with Luke inside laughing hysterically. Nothing could make this two-year-old unlock the door. This is one of those times it's great to have an athletic wife. When she was in high school and college Carrie was on softball teams. She was great at throwing, but was famous for her fast running. So my wife jumped over the deck gate, ran down the deck stairs and raced around the house at lightening speed to open the garage door before he could lock that one too. ...and just like that I was back on schedule.

Lydia recently took up a new hobby of hiding toys down her

pants. It's comical to see how many items she can cram in there, until recently when she got my E-Key for the I-Boxes (digital lockboxes). I had just set it down next to me while I put on my dress shoes. When I was ready to walk out the door I couldn't find it. I sure *thought* I laid it next to me. And there was Lydia, announcing she went pee pee in her pants. Sure enough, my E-Key was in her favorite hiding place. Thank goodness I had those disinfectant wipes in the car!

MAKE YOURSELF AVAILABLE WHEN YOUR PHONE RINGS

How self-sacrificing are you with your time for your clients? As one sells more and more properties, it gets tough to balance work with personal time. Every vacation my family has taken I have worked or at least made myself available for calls (by my choice). Odd as it may sound, that's a good thing. Since you can take a phone and laptop anywhere, and every hotel has a fax machine, it's easy to work from anywhere you go. Usually it takes just a few minutes here and there to still be available. I sold a house while sitting on the beach at Sanibel Island five years ago. I tried not to let the buyer's agent know I wasn't in town. After a few minutes she asked "What is that loud crashing noise I keep hearing?" I paused for a moment before informing her it was "ocean waves." I could sense her sound of envy. Perhaps I fueled it further when I said I was taking notes in the sand!

I've worked while vacationing in New York City. I remember talking on the phone while walking through Chinatown. I also negotiated a deal late one night while standing in Times Square. These calls usually take all of ten minutes, and I'm always available to take them. Does it bother me? No. Wear me out, yes. Sometimes during the busy spring market I'll be on a call, and by the time I hang up I have five new voice messages. While I'm listening to those messages I get even more calls! Days like that are way too hectic and stressful, but that also means your dreams are coming true because you're selling a lot of homes.

THIS BUSINESS IS FEAST OR FAMINE

I clearly remember the difficult famine during my earliest years as a realtor. Even though the feasting is stressful at times too, it has fantastic rewards. When I get so overworked that I feel I need two of me that day, I remind myself how horribly slow my first two years were, and I quickly become grateful to be so busy. The biggest difference I've noticed while working with hundreds of other agents on various transactions is the agents I want to work with again and again are always available. They work hard to find solutions to problems and the flow of communication is healthy and efficient.

Being available to your existing customers and returning calls immediately will lead to great working relationships. It will also keep you from losing your listings should they expire. Always being available will set you apart from other realtors and help make you a success. Your reaction when the phone rings and you really don't want to answer, will let your spouse and kids know your level of commitment. You want to demonstrate that all calls are important to your success.

I've noticed recently that sometimes I sigh loudly when the phone rings at inconvenient times and sometimes I even make mean faces at the phone when it rings during dinner. We noticed our 4-year-old doing the same things last week, so I've stopped. I don't want my occasional irritation to become family resentment from my kids when the phone rings. The more positive I am in front of my family when the phone rings, the more supportive they'll be. If you have the support and encouragement of your spouse and children, you will thrive and become a bigger success than you ever dreamed.

#19 THERE ARE TIMES WHEN IT'S NOT NICE TO LAUGH AT OTHERS, OUT LOUD

WHEN THINGS ARE NOT GOING our way, it wears on us. Negativity from other people asking how much longer we'll be pursuing this real estate thing naturally irritates us. During a tough market when sales are lower than expected, the best way to overcome depression is to laugh. I laugh at myself constantly it seems, but I've learned the hard way that it's really not nice to laugh at others... out loud.

One morning I showed a family some homes and then took a break for lunch. While we ate, I listened to them discuss the first houses we saw, and then we went to see the final three homes. After viewing all of the homes, they decided to make an offer. We rushed back to my office and went in the front conference room. I was on page two of the contract when I swear I heard the husband pass gas. I should say at this point, it took all the self-discipline skills I've learned from self-help books not to die of laughter. I controlled myself and didn't even look his way. I continued with the contract as if nothing had happened, but somewhere around page five another fart noise came from the husband's side of the table. Nobody looked up. Nobody said a word. I continued, but as I turned paged six, he *really* let one, and his wife immediately looked up and said, "Would you stop it?! I can't believe you keep doing that while we're buying a house!"

He looked totally embarrassed and said he didn't think we could hear. At that point I tried very hard not to laugh. I stopped talking for a moment, afraid that if I opened my mouth I'd burst out laughing. We all sat there for a moment and then he said very calmly. "Do you have a bathroom?" His wife went outside to smoke while he went to the restroom, and I sat in the conference room laughing hysterically. And yes, they did buy a house.

A middle-aged woman was referred to me by a satisfied client. I was driving her around in my car showing her some properties for sale on a fairly warm winter day. She was wearing a lot of layers – a couple of shirts, a sweater and a heavy coat. After the second home, she began to complain how hot it was driving around so she threw her coat in the backseat. I turned down the heater. By the fourth home she was sweating and having a tough time. I lowered the windows and turned down the heat so low I was freezing. By the time we saw the last house she was fanning herself. Sweat was running down the sides of her face. As I was driving her back to her car with all the windows down, she was still complaining about how hot she was. At that point she decided to give me way too much information on menopause and the new medication she had just started taking and how she had never experienced hot flashes of such intensity. Her friends had warned her she might get flashes, but she had no idea they would be so intense and long lasting. She said she never thought she would be bearing her soul to a stranger, much less a guy, but she thought I should know what was wrong with her. For some reason, it then occurred to me I had accidentally left her heated seat turned on HIGH the whole time. When she finished sharing her medical history with me I sheepishly reached down to turn off the switch. She did not look pleased, and I never heard from her again. She did not buy a house – at least not from me!

NUDITY IS NOT SOMETHING TO LAUGH AT

When we had our previous home for sale in 2006, I learned to empathize with the sellers who must keep their homes looking perfect at all times in case of a showing. One day we got a request for a showing on our own house. The inside was perfect and ready to show (we didn't have children at that point), and I wanted our beautiful yard to look its best, so I went home to mow really fast. I even mowed the front yard in two directions so it had a nice pattern in the grass from the perfect mow lines. I was soaked with sweat from mowing so fast but since I still had about 45 minutes before the showing, I went in to get cleaned up so I could get out in time. Our house was a ranch with the laundry room at the far end by the kitchen, so I went in there and stripped all the way down tossing my sweaty clothes in the washing machine. Then I walked through the house to take a shower. We had a beautiful leaded glass front door with extra glass on the sides - lots of glass and no blinds. As I stepped in the entryway, I glanced at the front door and realized that the agent and her buyers were there – 45 minutes early! She was unlocking the door! I don't know if it was the sweat under my feet or the fact that my heart rate tripled in a split second, but I slid on the tile entry floor and fell down …naked. Very similar to the story in the beautiful home earlier, but with no snow and much fewer clothes. I leaped up, dashed into my closet and within seconds put on shorts and an old shirt that was definitely a size too small. I squeezed it down around my neck, backwards I later learned, and ran back to the entryway to escape. No socks, no shoes, messy hair and soaked with sweat. I quickly left saying goodbye, but making no eye contact. I couldn't look them in the face knowing they must have watched me fall down in the entryway. I drove off barefoot really wishing I'd never mowed the yard that day. No, they did not buy the house.

SOMETIMES THE OBVIOUS IS BEST LEFT UNSAID

I showed a small home (not one of my personal listings) to some investor friends of mine. The home had two very small bedrooms with a living room, a small kitchen and one bathroom. No garage and no basement. It was a good price range for my investor friends to purchase for rental property. The home sounded great in the computer, so I was certain they would want it. So all of us arrived at this house, both investor friends and their wives, and yet another friend who would be looking for inspection items in need of fixing. One of them even brought his parents. The eight of us stood in the front yard of this investment opportunity as I unlocked the door. This was definitely one of those times when the listing agent should have talked with the owners about how to show their home. It was absolutely the filthiest house I'd ever been in. The smell! To the right of the living room was the kitchen with dirty dishes from the past week piled everywhere. Old pans of food were on the stove and dog dishes were on the floor next to a huge bag of spilled dog food. Piles of dirty clothes were in the living room next to a half-filled fish tank of stagnant water. The whole house smelled like body odor and dog feces! Had these been renters, we might have understood, but the actual homeowners lived in the house. We loudly criticized how some people live like animals. They must have had a baby by the looks of the toys on the floor. We continued to loudly comment on the filth and foul stench that permeated this gross home. We continued with the tour as we glanced at the smallest bedroom and the filthy nasty bathroom. At that point we were so disgusted, trying not to touch anything, that we were all joking loudly about what nasty people these must be and how unfortunate for their baby to be raised by such barbaric parents. Then we all went in the master bedroom. Somehow they had squeezed a king sized mattress into this small room with only about a foot of clearance all the way around.

One of my investor friends went in first and I followed. I'm not sure why but we all squeezed in around the mattress. This was perhaps the grossest room with piles of stinky dirty clothes on the mattress, bags of donuts and a half eaten pizza on the night stand. My friend's mom said in a loud authoritative tone, "This is disgusting! I could just vomit. I can't stand to be in this nasty house anymore!"

That's when somebody moved under the sheets and piles of dirty clothes on the bed. We all jumped from the shock, at the same instant two of my friends yelled "#&@%!" The friend who had gone in first was trapped being farthest from the door. He instinctively removed himself from the situation by stepping on the mattress, jumping over the person, running out of the room. The rest of us struggled to squeeze out the door as fast as possible, probably from the shame we felt from being so loud and critical. Those poor homeowners certainly needed staging!

#20 Did Your Real Estate Classes Prepare You to Be a Counselor and Therapist?

AT THE END OF MY senior year in high school, I knew my race around the track was coming to a close. All my finals were completed, I had run the hurdles for the last time and I could slow down knowing the finish line was coming. It was time for graduation. Both of my grandmothers traveled here for commencement. Since they came especially to see me, my parents thought I should spend some quality time with both of them. I decided to take them to a museum the morning of my graduation. Let me say I was blessed with two pretty amazing grandmothers. Both were hardworking strong Christian women who were great role models. My mom's mom, Grandma Franks, was very hard of hearing, especially during her later years. She wore hearing aids in both ears and had developed a habit of talking a little too loud especially in public. She was in good health, but slow-moving and cautious with her walking. Dad's mom was "Mamu." Mamu was short and very spunky. She had lots of energy and she loved people. She made friends with everyone she would meet.

The three of us entered the museum at a snail's pace due to Grandma Franks' walking, which frustrated Mamu to no end. I was trying to slow Mamu down, while trying to stay close to Grandma Franks. It became clear that Mamu could whip through a whole section of the museum within minutes, only taking a quick glance at half the items. On the other hand, Grandma Franks enjoyed reading the detailed description of each item. I quickly hurried to check on Mamu who was far ahead happily chatting with one of the guards. Just as I went back to find Grandma Franks, I heard a loud male voice from around the corner saying, "Ma'am please don't touch the tapestry." As I turned the corner I found Grandma Franks reaching up tugging on the corner of a huge priceless tapestry. I could hear Grandma talking out loud to herself, "Amazing stitching on this! Just marvelous!"

The guard yelled from the far end of the hallway again, "Lady, I said turn loose of the tapestry!" Grandma Franks couldn't hear a word, and she lifted the corner up even more to get a really close look. This enormous tapestry must have been hundreds of years old perhaps from an old castle in Europe. I hesitated to yell because I was sure loud talking of any kind was forbidden, but I needed her to hear me. I think the next few moments went something like this: I said loudly, "Grandma, you can't touch the tapestry."

People in other parts of the museum all turned our direction, as Grandma replied louder, "You say you want to touch this tapestry?"

"No Grandma," I said much louder, "Don't touch the tapestry!"

"What?" Grandma said even louder.

"You both need to back away from the tapestry!" yelled the guard as he hurried towards us. Within seconds two guards were standing beside us. Grandma said to all of us, "Now look here. I want to show you this beautiful stitching. Did you know this is over 400 years old?" And as she reached for it again, both guards said "Ma'am please don't touch the tapestry!" I started laughing because I could tell she couldn't hear. She started laughing too as she fiddled with one of her hearing aids. At this point more people in the museum had come to watch the commotion.

I said in a normal voice while she read my lips, "No Grandma, do not touch." Grandma turned to the guards, "Well, if you didn't want me to touch it then why is it out here in the open for people to touch? You should have it roped off! Now, I want you to see this stitching. They just don't make things like this anymore." Grandma Franks finally turned loose of the tapestry and we slowly continued our tour. She seemed perplexed what the big fuss was about. She continued to talk loudly the whole time about how exceptional that stitching was and how she wished she could sew like that. Grandma Franks loved to learn and she probably could have spent an hour in each room.

At that moment I realized I had lost Mamu. I didn't know where to start looking, but I didn't want to leave Grandma Franks and lose both of them, so Grandma Franks and I took quite a while walking to the other end of the museum at her slow pace. There was no Mamu to be found! We took the elevator upstairs where there was a beautiful exhibit of relics from some ancient dynasty. There was a particularly ornate hand carved royal chair on display – and Mamu was sitting in it! I raced over to her and said "Mamu, you can't sit here! This chair is probably 1000 years old!"

She responded back in the most irritated tone, "Well sam hill, I've been up here for half an hour and there isn't anybody to talk to and the bunions on my feet are killing me. This chair is the most uncomfortable thing I've ever seen. I've been through this whole museum and there's nothing here worth looking at so we can all go home." I agreed, so we started the very slow walk back out.

It was a fascinating study of two people in the same place, at the same time, reacting completely differently to their surroundings. How typical this is on a listing appointment when the husband and wife are not even close to being on the same page when it comes to selling their house.

The personal information that complete strangers will reveal is astonishing. Many of our clients are going through bad times and, unfortunately, that's the reason they are selling their home. Sometimes elderly people are moving to a retirement center and the rest of the family is there to help fill out listing papers. If the elderly homeowner doesn't want to sell, it can be a very difficult day for everyone. You may hear two hours of memories while the owner fills out the seller's disclosure, but that is part of your job – to listen. It's an emotional time when people sell their homes, especially if they really don't want to sell. Some of my clients have sat and wept because they are so overwhelmed with the burdens they're facing.

Nobody wants to go into foreclosure, but in this tough market many people are. If your sellers are facing major financial problems, your listing appointment will be difficult as you listen to what they are going through. I've also been on appointments where they hoped the best solution was to sell their house, but after listening to everything going on in their lives, I knew there was just no way they could handle the stress of selling. At one listing appointment, I found out from one spouse that a divorce was coming BEFORE THE OTHER SPOUSE KNEW. Even when appointments don't result in listing the house, we find ourselves caught up in very real lives of people just by listening to all they have going on. I've had people needing to quickly sell a home to pay medical bills for a very sick child. Another family needed to move from a split-level to a ranch because the wife was on chemotherapy and soon would not have the strength to walk up flights of stairs.

People are overwhelmed with burdens, and sometimes we are placed in their lives simply to give them encouragement and hope. There are few other jobs out there where we can be used to offer hope and encouragement. Many of my clients just need someone to listen to them, to pray for them. It's okay not to have answers and solutions for everyone; sometimes they just need a friend to talk to, and I believe sometimes we're placed in these people's lives at that moment just to let them know someone cares. Even if you don't list the house and you don't get a new buyer, you can be someone of significance to a total stranger in desperate need of a friend.

#21 How to Do an Amazingly Successful Open House:

YOU CAN JUST SHOW UP at your open house, or you can put some hard work into preparing for it. This is how you do an open house when you desperately need to pick up more buyers. Pick a good listing in an area where you want buyers to hold an open house, even if it's not your listing. First, get the listing agent's permission and make a new flyer about the house with *your* name and *your* phone number on it. Use those only during the open house, and don't leave any in the house after you leave. Remember you are there to sell *this* property, but chances are the people coming into the open house will not be buying it. Even though your goal at an open house is to sell the house you're in, you can also find out what these buyers are really looking for, so you may be able to sell them a different house. Either way you have a new buyer, and soon you will have income. During my first few weeks, I went to many open houses just to observe how other agents did it. I learned a lot!

First, show up early. Get permission from the listing agent to start your open house an hour earlier than normal and stay late. The longer you have it open to the public, the more opportunity to get people in the door.

Make sure you contact the listing agent when you are finished to give a report on how many people came and what their comments were. The homeowners will want to know how successful the open house was as soon as they come home. Make sure the homeowners and listing agent are pleased with the job you did, because it's possible you'll hold the same house open again the following Sunday. If you are holding a vacant house open, you need to get there early enough to turn on the A/C or furnace so it's comfortable. Take a roll of toilet paper in case there is none in the house.

Make new flyers or handouts with the details on the house you're in, and remember, with *your* name, phone number and picture. Then make a separate flyer about *you*. You need something to market yourself and the company you work for. You can use this same flyer about yourself for a variety of different open houses. List reasons why a potential buyer should use you as their agent. Maybe you grew up in the area around your open house? Maybe you went to college or high school nearby? List all the positives about your company and why you work for them. Perhaps you have a special online tool to help the buyer, and you just need their email address to get them started. Advertise that on your flyer. As people come in give them both flyers. If they are not buying this house, then they'll throw away the house flyer immediately, but they may just keep your personal flyer. Use your headshot, and possibly another photo of you standing with a Sold sign at the bottom.

Have a notepad with you at all times to take notes during the open house. As potential buyers walk in, they will introduce themselves that one time. Immediately write down their names. If their kids are older, introduce yourself to them too, and write down their names.

Don't be too aggressive or pushy, and don't follow them all over the house interviewing them. Let them look in peace. After they've looked around a bit, begin asking what they think and let the conversation develop with them doing most of the talking. You need for them to tell you what exactly they're looking for and why. Many times a buyer cannot afford the house you're holding open, so find out their price range. How fast are they looking to move? Are they preapproved? Before you get too involved in a conversation, find out if they are working with another realtor. If they are, they will usually tell you as soon as they walk in the door so they can avoid your sales pitch, but most don't have an agent. That's why they're out looking at open houses by themselves.

I pick up new clients from open houses on a regular basis because I am relaxed with them. I don't follow them around bugging them. I have flyers for them to take (the one about the house and the one about me), which I hand them as they come into the kitchen. Sometimes I also have a flyer from a loan officer showing different mortgage options. Many times potential buyers will be surprised that the house is more affordable than they think.

You should have a sheet where people sign in. Some people don't want to give their address, because in actuality they are neighbors from four houses away and just wanted to see inside the house. Don't pressure to get an address. But with the addresses you do get, write a note thanking them for coming and insert your business card. Keep it short. "Mr. and Mrs. Jones, Thank you for stopping by my open house yesterday. It was very nice meeting you. Feel free to call me if I can ever be of assistance in serving your real estate needs." Write your name so they can read it, along with your phone number. It helps to have the thank you cards, envelopes and stamps with you. Fill them out at the end of your open house and then go mail them. Your work is done!

If it's raining outside, take towels with you. Don't use the homeowner's towels. Lay your towels by the front door with your own shoes on them. You'll find everybody coming in will automatically take their shoes off too. All of these potential buyers will notice how you conduct your open house. They are all interested in moving, maybe not in the near future and maybe not in that price range, but they have the hopes of moving.

The better you are at conducting open houses the higher your chances of picking up new clients.

OPEN HOUSE DIRECTIONAL SIGNS

If I'm out showing houses on a Sunday and we're going from house to house, we'll come across occasional open houses. I'm amazed that many agents put out so few open house directional signs that I can't even find the house. I have to admit when I do an open house, I dislike placing signs the most. Stopping the car, getting out, putting the sign in the ground, getting back in, and then on to the next corner. It's really a nuisance to deal with week after week, but common sense would tell us that the more open house directional signs out there, the better. If there are two neighborhood entrances, then obviously you should put open directionals at all the turns leading in from both ways. Maybe your office gives you a couple of free signs when you first join, but you're going to need more. I have 18 open directionals. And since I had to pay for them, I put my name in large caps all across the top of each sign. If you can get that much free advertising for three hours every Sunday, you'll start putting them on every corner.

WALKING DOOR-TO-DOOR BEFOREHAND

This is what really sets apart the hard-working agents from all the others. If you need potential clients, then the more people who come through your open house, the better your chances of picking up a new client.

If you want to maximize your marketing, create a flyer about yourself and the house. If your open house is on Sunday, then you should go door to door (knocking on every door) to all the homes around your upcoming open house. You have a reason to talk with them in person. I would say, "Hi, my name is Jonathan

Goforth. I'm a realtor with Reece & Nichols and I just wanted to let you know I'm having this house open tomorrow." Pointing towards the house you're having open. Hand them a flyer with *your* name and headshot large at the bottom and a picture of the house at the top. Keep in mind this is probably not your listing, so get permission from the listing agent to do this. Then tell the neighbor, "Feel free to stop by or invite anyone you might know who is thinking of moving to the area. Thanks for your time." Keep it short and move to the next house. Usually they will say, "Thanks" and shut the door. But many times, they'll ask questions about that house. "How much are they asking?" "Are you getting much activity?" "Where are they moving to?" "You know we had some friends over last night and they were asking about that house for sale. I'll go call them." "What time is your open house?" Remember the bottom line, "The more people who know you sell houses, the more houses you will sell."

Let's say that you have the house open on the next day from 1-4pm – and nobody comes. Think how good you'll still feel knowing you went to the surrounding 40 homes advertising yourself the day before. The more seeds you plant, the higher your chances of a really good harvest.

PUT AN "OPEN SUNDAY" RIDER ON THE FOR SALE SIGN DURING THE WEEK

Your office should have Open Sunday riders. You can even put the time range on the Open Sunday rider. If it says Open Sunday 1-4pm, be in place before 1pm, with all your open directionals in place and all the lights on. You should also put an open directional sign in the yard so people know you are there and inviting them in. Balloons are always a nice touch. The better your preparation and marketing for each open house, the better your chance of success. The key is consistency. Hold open houses as often as you can. If you have no business, then conduct an open house every Sunday until you get buyers. The latest trend is doing open houses on Saturdays also. Be open to trying new things. See what works and do those things consistently.

ALWAYS USE PROTECTION

I have never had a safety problem doing an open house, but on occasion we hear of agents getting robbed during an open house. Make sure your spouse or a friend always knows the address of the house you are holding open. If you feel unsafe doing open houses, position yourself where you can watch to see who is walking up before they get to the door. That way you are prepared to open the door for them. If for some reason you are uncomfortable with somebody about to come inside, you should step outside as if you're leaving as they approach. Act like you're making a call and stand in the front yard where neighbors can easily see. That removes you from the house until you decide what to do. You can also take a spouse or friend with you if you feel uncomfortable.

I never go to the basement or other secluded areas with potential buyers. If they need me to answer a question, I stand in the hallway and reply from there. I always hold paper and pen with me to take notes, but I also hold my phone in case I need to make an emergency call. Some realtors carry mace but I've never felt that need. I guess if I ever felt so uncomfortable that I thought I needed protection of that kind, I probably wouldn't have held that particular house open. Use your instincts and common sense as to how you conduct an open house.

Before we had kids, my wife, Carrie, would frequently come to open houses with me. It was a great time to hang out together and she enjoyed getting caught up on magazine reading. With kids in the family now, it's more challenging, but sometimes she brings the kids by for a few minutes, especially if it's a home she wants to view. This usually works pretty well, except for one open house last summer.

This open house had beautiful flowers growing along the front walkway. Earlier that spring Lydia and Luke had thoroughly enjoyed pulling off all the blooms from the petunias on our deck. Those little plants didn't even get a good start before we had to throw them all away. We knew they enjoyed picking flowers, but when they saw the abundance of beautiful blooms at this house, they quickly stripped two of those plants entirely clean of every bloom. Dozens of little wadded up flowers were thrown all over the concrete. As we grabbed Luke and rushed him to the van, Lydia, way ahead of her years with wisdom, realized she had little time left. She began yanking entire plants out of the ground – shaking dirt from their roots all over the walkway. AGHHH! So much damage in such little time! Carrie took them home while I stayed and tried to replant their front landscaping before the open house was over. The homeowners arrived finding me hosing off their concrete and watering their plants. They didn't ask, and I didn't tell.

I have heard that if you bake cookies or bread you'll sell the house. Well, I have baked cookies a few times during opens. I bought a huge tub of cookie dough, took my own cookie sheet, and baked just enough to make the house smell good. That's a lot of effort and organization for me, especially when I don't like to cook. At one open house I was baking cookies and the buzzer went off signaling that the cookies were done. Unfortunately the doorbell rang at the same time, and I answered it first. By the time I got the cookies out, I had a burned cookie smell all over the house. I stopped baking cookies after that, and I started taking a scented candle instead. Remember when I was new in real estate I asked for stamps for Christmas? Since nobody really wanted to give me stamps, I also asked for candles one year – something that would smell like cookies or bread. I got one and I used that candle for almost two years at open houses.

Early in my real estate career I had a board call to have an agent discuss what would be involved in listing their home. I had never been on a listing appointment with people I'd never met before, so I asked my broker to go with me. She did. It was a good meeting and near the end, these clients asked me to list their house. Wow!

I met them by myself the next afternoon to have them sign the listing papers. I took the pictures, measured the rooms and asked if I could hold open houses. They were very gracious to let me do an open house for 7 weeks in a row. I did everything possible to market the open houses. I hung door hangers on all the neighbor's houses advertising the open house each week - with my name and phone number. I put "Open Sunday" on the For Sale sign during the week in the hopes people driving by might come back on Sunday. I even put "Open Sunday from 1-5pm" on each flyer in the flyer box hanging on the For Sale sign. I ran an ad in the newspaper and another online.

Of those open houses seven weeks in a row, the first three weeks nobody came. Nobody. The fourth week, I had many groups come through. On that Sunday two different couples who didn't like that particular house let me show them other houses. During the weeks following, another family let me show them other homes, and they did buy a house from me.

It was the seventh open house when a couple stopped by who wanted to build a brand new house. They were out looking at lots in a nearby neighborhood, and just stopped by my open house for fun. They took their time and walked through the home. I gave them my flyers and let them look in peace. They informed me they had a buyer's agent helping them already, but how they really wanted to build a new house instead. They stayed a long time as other people came and went, listening to how I talked about the home to other lookers. Before they left, Mrs. Buyer said they thought they wanted to buy my open house. I asked if I could call their agent, which I did while they were there. Two nights later their agent showed it to them again and they bought the house!

What happened next was amazing. Their agent was only part time and had a full-time job as a nurse. The buyers needed to sell their existing home in order to purchase this one, but they didn't want her to be their listing agent on their current home due to her lack of availability. They informed me they had been interviewing other agents to list their old house and had decided to choose me. I made sure their agent was aware, and she was completely supportive of it. When I asked why they picked me, they said they were so impressed with how I handled that open house that they were sold on *me*. Are you keeping track of the success from this first board call?

I sold these clients' old house and they closed on my listing, and over the next year they referred me to four of their friends. I sold those friends' houses too. The following year the family across the street from the original open house called me to come and just give a price opinion on their house. They might want to sell; they might not. While I was there they decided to go ahead and list their house with me. Thank goodness I had a listing packet with me! When I asked why they had originally called me, they showed me one of those open house door hangers I had put on their front door a year earlier – with my name and phone number. Months after my original listing had sold across the street, the door hanger paid off!

Not only did I sell that house, but I also sold their son's house later that year also. Their son has since referred me to two of his friends. When their son got married, I relisted the house I sold him and then sold his wife and him another house.

Five years later I heard from the people who bought the original house I had listed. They wanted to sell the house to finally build a new house – in another state. So I listed the house again and referred them to an agent in that state who gladly paid a referral fee. All of this started from a board call and seven open houses. None of these clients were in my community of influence; all of them strangers to me. Guess how much income this generated? $57,200! Not bad for one board call.

You simply never know when a board call or an open house or hanging flyers on neighbors' doorknobs will lead to success. Open houses work! And these are very inexpensive ways of getting business. If you are brand new and have no money for mailings, and no community of influence, and no connections with builders or developers, and really have almost no family or friends of any kind – you can still succeed!

#22 Stay Up Late and Sleep In

FOR ME, THE SCHEDULE AND flexibility of being a Realtor is perfect. I still enjoy staying up until the wee hours of the morning, and if I wake up before seeing the *Showcase Showdown* on "The Price is Right," it's too early to get up.

What other job in the world lets you sleep in as long as you want every day and still be financially successful? Think back to a past job you've had. Let's say it's a dreary morning in early October - you woke up late because it was pouring rain outside. You jumped in the car hoping to speed to work but due to the heavy rain, traffic on the highway was barely moving. You got to work late, and wet, and in a bad mood. This is exactly the type of day you wished you could've stayed home in bed sleeping. Have you ever had a day like this? After you ate lunch at your desk you didn't get much work done because you were dragging and wishing you could go home to take a nap? Well, that's what I do! I encourage you to do the same. If you want to take a nap and you have no appointments …then go home and take a nap. Enjoy the flexibility this career gives you.

Being a realtor gives you flexibility that no other career can offer. I can participate so much more in raising our children. I can work out at a gym during the day when it's not so crowded. I can eat lunch with my friends and I don't feel the pressure of having to hurry back to a job where I might get chewed out for being late. The only people you need to be accountable to is yourself, your family, your broker, and your clients. The negatives of this flexibility are that only a very self-disciplined and self-driven person will succeed because the main person you need to be accountable to is... yourself. As you get busy showing property and juggling paperwork on many transactions you'll find you're working lots of odd hours. I find myself working many evenings and weekends. It's the nature of the job – but when I worked retail jobs years ago, I had the very same hours. I worked many evenings and weekends... and almost every holiday. Not much has really changed except my name and picture are hanging on 1000 refrigerators and I believe I make a little more income.

ENJOY THE FLEXIBILITY THIS CAREER GIVES YOU

When I think about the advantages of being a realtor, compared to the limitations of a regular job, I work much harder at being a successful realtor so I never have to return to the corporate world. Take pride in what you do. No matter how frustrated you might become when you're not selling as many houses as you'd like, keep the attitude of "I'm going to make this work, or I'm going to die trying." Give it everything you can until the day comes you realize that you've stepped over that line drawn before you. Life will never be like it was before, and you'll enjoy the wonderfully unique lifestyle selling real estate will provide.

#23 Stack Up the Brush, Apply Lighter Fluid and Strike a Match

IT'S TIME TO CREATE AN ACTION PLAN to build your real estate business. Maybe your broker calls it a business plan or a marketing plan, but whatever label you want to give it, you need a check list of what to do. Your broker is there to help you. Every single thing your broker does has the ultimate goal of helping *you* be a success, so make sure they are aware how seriously you are taking this business.

I believe in a tough market you should have two goals: First you need to make enough money to pay your bills and expenses. These are your *needs*. Basically, this is the minimum amount of income you must have to continue as a realtor. Then there is the more ambitious goal of reaching your *wants*. Why is this important? Because in a tough market, agents are quitting. Why? They did not put in enough work to reach their goals. They began the year without an action plan to achieve success. If you only need to make $60,000/year to pay taxes and all your bills, then you don't need to make $150,000 to survive. But if you *do* need to make $60,000/year to continue your current lifestyle, then you still need to be selling quite a few homes.

At the beginning of each year, my broker asks each agent to list our estimated sales for that year – How many houses we plan to sell, broken down between how many listings and how many buyers we will need to achieve that goal. We estimate an average price range to forecast our total volume and therefore our income. What is your income goal over the next 12 months? Would $30,000 income be enough? Let's say it would take approximately $1.5 million in sales volume to make that much money. If your average house might sell for $150,000, then you need to sell about 10 homes. Or if you're fortunate to sell a higher price range, then you only have to sell five homes at $300,000 each. The point of this is to help you realize you don't need to be overwhelmed by thinking you need to sell 200 houses each year to achieve your goal.

Take this a step further. In a tough market, all of your listings will not sell. Some will be priced too high, and the sellers cannot reduce. After a while some will get rented and some might go into foreclosure. A few homeowners will remove their houses from the market planning to try again in the future hoping the market isn't so saturated. And occasionally you'll keep a listing for many months, possibly over a year, and it sells way in the future. Let's say of the 10 houses you need to sell this year, you expect 5 of them to be listings, and 5 to be buyers. How many houses do you need to list to get those 5 to actually sell? Possibly 8? Maybe more? It all depends on location, price, condition and what that house has to offer compared to the competition. How sellable is that house when you take on that listing?

LISTINGS ARE VITAL TO YOUR SUCCESS

It's interesting to me how important Listings are to our long-term success. They will ensure your survival in this business. It's true: "You have to List to last". Most of my business comes from getting listings, but many of my listings are not selling in this market. So in order to pay my bills, I need to list *more* houses than ever before to find the ones that <u>will</u> sell. To be honest, when it comes to estimating how many houses you're going to sell this year, nobody really knows. You can't write down a magic number and expect it to just come true. Every house you sell won't be at your estimated price, and you won't have the same number of buyers and sellers. It's a guessing game looking into the future, but do understand this: You don't need to sell the whole city to be a success. Your goal setting should come as a relief when you see you only need to sell around $1.5 million to be satisfied and continue on for another year.

How many houses sold in your general area last year? Let's say your area had around 3,000 houses sell in the past 12 months. (It could be much higher than that depending on the metropolitan area). Of those 3,000 houses, don't you think you could sell 10? How hard would that be? Wouldn't it be just as possible for you to sell 50? Can you imagine the income if you sold 50 houses in a year? The fact is, if over 3,000 houses sold in your part of the metro area, then a lot of people are selling a lot of houses – in a tough market. Lots of houses are selling right now, and lots of houses will sell this next year too. Lots of houses will sell the year after that, and you just need to find your 10 houses to get in on that market.

I want you to be reassured, before getting frustrated, that you can be a success in real estate. If you have the desire, strong work ethic, and the ability to self-motivate yourself …you'll sell those 10 houses, likely even more, and you'll be able to pay your bills and live your chosen lifestyle. The Action Plan to create business will work for you just as it has worked for me. If you sell 10 houses this year in a tough market, then you'll very likely sell more than 10 the following year. You're investing in a long-term plan to create a lifestyle very few other realtors have.

PLAN WHAT YOU ARE GOING TO DO

While you might not be able to estimate the exact number of houses you're going to sell this year, you can control how much money you are going to spend marketing yourself as a real estate agent. How many of the suggestions in this book will you follow? How many training classes are you going to take? Is this the year you get a new designation? Are you going to join any new organizations this year to meet people? Are you going to conduct an email marketing campaign? Are you going to make some phone calls? Will you order customized For Sale signs with your picture? Do you need a new headshot? Do you plaster your name all over your car? Are you going to put in the extra effort to conduct successful open houses?

Are you going to send any mailings to your COI list? If so, what should you plan on sending? There are so many ways to spend money on marketing it's truly amazing. I've even heard you can put your name and picture on those sanitation disks you see in men's bathrooms to pee on! You can advertise on grocery carts, in the newspaper and all over the internet. It's endless, and you can spend millions of dollars doing it. How do you plan to spend money marketing yourself this year?

CREATE YOUR ACTION PLAN TO GET FROM POINT A TO POINT B

Take out a piece of paper and make a list of what you will do this week. Start with something simple like sending a mailing with a "free market analysis certificate" included. Make a list of what you plan to do over the next month, the next six months, and for the remainder of the year. How many open houses will you do? Pick one for this coming Sunday and get your personal flyer ready to hand out with the info on the home. Get your customized door hangers ready to market to the neighbors.

YOU NEED TO BUILD A FIRE

Sometimes it's hard to start a fire with wet wood, but if you prospect correctly from the beginning and stay consistent, you'll create a blaze so strong that even a tough market will not extinguish your fire.

Even if you were selling a lot more houses a few years ago, your business should not collapse in a tough market. If you are continuing to prospect effectively, than the glowing embers you still have in your brush pile should be smoldering and waiting for new dry wood. If you are brand new to building a real estate business then you need to build a fire that will be hard to put out. You must learn how to sell homes in a tough market.

Building this fire is similar to creating your Action Plan. You'll need to do some preparation before lighting the match though. Not a lot really, but you must have a plan before you begin. First stack up some brush. Apply dead grass, little twigs and small branches throughout it. Would a rake help? Now you are getting prepared with making a checklist of what to do.

On the other hand, if you simply light a field of tall dead grass with old limbs randomly scattered, the grass will burn so fast from underneath that the limbs won't catch on fire. You will have burned up the entire field of grass, possibly spreading to other neighboring fields causing disaster. In the meantime all the dead grass and twigs are gone so there is no kindling left to start a new fire.

If you have a plan before you begin, either in building fires or real estate sales, then you'll likely be blessed with a successful outcome every time. The key to building a fire, or becoming a top selling realtor, is to follow the action plan exactly.

You Must Also Be Thinking Ahead

I would suggest a garden hose too. You certainly don't want to catch the surrounding grass and trees on fire. You don't want distractions taking you away from being effective and productive on burning your brush pile. You'll need matches and lighter fluid to save time and build momentum. Timing is crucial so you'll need a dry day with as little wind as possible. Watch the weather in advance so you are prepared for the best day to start your fire. Stack up the brush and dead grass. Turn on the hose first to help direct your efforts ...and if your brush pile is large, you might call a few friends to come and help. Those friends and their phone numbers should be listed in your Center of Influence list (List A). If you made a check list before beginning, then you're ready. That "check list" is your Action Plan for building a successful fire. It's time to stack up the brush, apply lighter fluid and strike a match!

Make a check list of all the things you will do over the next few days and weeks to become a successful real estate agent. It's time to organize your to-do list into your action plan. It's your time to sell real estate!

#24 12-WEEK ACTION PLAN TO SELL A HOME!

Seller's Name: _____

Address: _____

Listing Date: _____

WEEK 1:

- ✓ Before going to your listing appointment, take a picture of the front of the home and use it in your listing presentation. Make a flyer promoting you and the home using the picture saying SOLD to begin your presentation.
- ✓ Prepare a CMA to help price the home. Inform the sellers as to how many other homes are for sale in the nearby area and also on a larger scale of the zip code. How many days on market is the average listing? How long will it take to sell the current inventory of homes? How many houses are under contract, and how long were those houses on the market? How many have been reduced? The better educated your sellers, the more effective you will be at pricing the home correctly.
- ✓ Take a resume showcasing information about <u>you</u>.
- ✓ Make sure you have a complete Listing Packet with you, including a calculator, camera, lockbox, tape measure, and

For Sale sign. I take my calculator and camera in with me when I arrive. I am prepared to fill out the Seller's Estimated Proceeds form, and my camera tells them I plan on taking pictures, which obviously means I plan on listing their home that night.

✓ Take notes as the homeowners show you around their home. This will help you market the home and write the remarks.

✓ As you fill out the listing forms, review all items that remain with the property. For example curtains and rods, decorative shelves, upgraded light fixtures, fountains, etc.

✓ Double check room sizes, taxes, schools, HOA fees and amenities.

✓ Make sure you have the seller's names correct on each form as they are listed on the tax record.

✓ Fill out the seller's estimated proceeds form with their accurate loan balance.

✓ If the sellers will owe money at closing make sure they understand that, and ask if they have the funds to bring to closing.

✓ Pick a Listing price and discuss potential future price reductions.

✓ Make sure you try the key before placing it in the lockbox.

✓ Place your customized For Sale sign in the yard, with a flyer box.

✓ Place directional signs on corners if they are allowed.

✓ Discuss staging if necessary, and ideas to help the home show better.

✓ Take pictures at that same time if the home is in "show condition". Make sure all lights are on, and your pictures are clear and of good quality. Take multiple shots of the same room to find the best angle.

✓ Make sure you have enough pictures for MLS, flyers and postcards.

✓ Plan Open Houses at that listing appointment, and mark calendar with dates.

✓ If your real estate company has a "Listing Alert" online program, load your new listing into it immediately to get the agents in your company showing it.

✓ Plan a Broker/Agent Tour and mark your calendar. Impress your sellers with all that you are doing to market their home.

✓ Have your office secretary load your new listing into MLS, and check the listing for accuracy.

✓ Load your pictures and make sure they are bright and clear so the home will look its best.

✓ Turn in all listing forms and documents to your office secretary.

✓ Put all of your listing papers in a folder to stay organized from the beginning.

✓ Load each of your seller's phone numbers into your cell phone so you have their numbers handy when you have questions and to call them with an offer.

✓ Look in MLS to see which agents are selling in this price range close by. Email or call them to network and ask them to show your new listing.

✓ Make sure your listing has downloaded from MLS onto your company website. Also check Realtor.com, Zillow.com and other websites to make sure it is downloading accurately.

✓ Create your marketing flyers and any literature to place inside the home. Give the homeowner extra copies so they can keep their flyer box from running out.

✓ Make 25 copies of the Seller's Disclosure and place them in the house with your flyers.

✓ Talk with sellers about the pros and cons of them having a pre-inspection.

✓ Order between 50-100qty "Just Listed" postcards and have them mailed to the surrounding homes.

✓ Order 50 unaddressed "Just Listed" postcards and give them to the sellers to distribute to people they know.

✓ Email a "Just Listed" flyer to 30 agents who have had recent sales in the area.

✓ Find out how many buyers are registered with saved searches this home fits into. Market your listing to those buyers and agents representing those buyers. Your company will likely have an online system in place for you to search for these clients already in place.

✓ Use MLS to search for every active home nearby. Send each listing agent the info on your new listing. As those agents get calls from potential buyers wanting to see their listing, those buyers might ask those agents what else is for sale. Remind those listing agents on a regular basis with the details about your house. Reverse marketing can be a powerful tool.

✓ Email and/or mail a flyer to your COI list advertising this new listing.

✓ Get your seller preapproved for their next purchase, if they will be buying another home.

✓ Load your sellers into an online "Sell My Home" type of system your company hopefully offers so your seller can track web hits, number of showings, housing data, etc.

✓ Also load your sellers into a program where they can begin looking at homes to purchase.

✓ Enter your new listing onto Craigslist and any other similar sites where buyers are searching.

✓ Hold your listing open the first weekend as suggested in Chapter 21, and write thank you notes to those who visited.

WEEK 2:

✓ Put your new listing on Broker Tour for agents to come view the home. If you are having food or offering a giveaway, take flyers to every real estate office nearby. Send an E-flyer to every nearby broker and agent with the details of your tour. Inform the sellers of the times for the tour so they can have their home clean and ready to show.

✓ If you are having lunch for agents, make sure you are in place early with everything set up, including your open directionals in place on street corners.

✓ Always use "feedback sheets" for agents to give suggestions. If you believe the house is overpriced or you need the sellers to clean carpets, declutter, or make changes to their home, feedback sheets can be a good tool for you. Agents can offer constructive criticism to your seller, offering good advice that you might not be able to say sometimes.

✓ Communicate with your sellers the responses from your Broker Tour. Discuss adjusting the price, or making improvements if you need to.

✓ Ask your seller if they have viewed the property online. Discuss the remarks in MLS with them to make sure they are pleased.

✓ Prepare for your next Open House.

WEEK 3:

✓ Have a lender make flyers for you to pass out showing various monthly payments depending on different down payments. Place these in the house also. This is creating another opportunity for you to communicate and see your sellers when you deliver the flyers.

✓ If your listing is overpriced but your sellers are reluctant to reduce, offer to personally show them comparable homes in the area so they can compare their home to the others. As you preview homes with your sellers ask them, "Would you pay as much as you're asking for your own house compared to these others?"

✓ Prepare for another open house, or ask agents in your office if anyone would like to hold it open for you.

WEEK 4:

✓ Check the placement of directional signs and the For Sale sign in the yard.

✓ Restock the flyer box on the sign.

✓ Create a new flyer online and distribute it to all your contacts.

✓ Rearrange the pictures and rewrite your remarks on MLS.

✓ Search for an updated list showing how many buyers are registered with saved searches this home fits into. Market your listing to those buyers and agents representing those buyers.

✓ Use MLS to search for every active home nearby. Send each listing agent the info on your new listing again. As those agents get calls from potential buyers wanting to see their listing, those buyers might ask those agents what else is for sale. Make sure you remind those listing agents frequently with the details on your house.

WEEK 5:

✓ Review MLS for new listings in the area. Are there any homes under contract? What did those homes have that yours doesn't? Have any other homes reduced their prices? Communicate this to your sellers.

✓ Re-check MLS listing to make sure it is accurate.

✓ Search other websites such as Trulia.com and Realtor.com to verify your listing is there.

✓ Create a new e-flyer and resend using your e-Marketing.

✓ If the house has not been reduced yet, this must be reviewed with the sellers. Offer, again, to show them comparable homes. Showing them their competition is not only the best way for them to accurately price their home, but gives you the opportunity to continue building a relationship with your sellers.

✓ Prepare for another open house. Go door-to-door each time marketing the open house to neighbors. Re-read Chapter 21 on how to conduct an amazingly successful open house.

✓ Re-enter your new listing onto Craigslist and any other similar sites where buyers are searching.

WEEK 6:

✓ Discuss creative incentives your sellers can offer a buyer. Perhaps they can offer a buy-down of the buyer's interest rate or offer to pay a certain portion of the buyer's closing costs.

✓ Take a new front picture and inside pictures if necessary.

✓ Update the flyer with new pictures.

✓ Check the placement of directional signs and the For Sale sign in the yard.

✓ Restock the flyer box on the sign.

✓ Verify that the seller has distributed all of their "new listing" postcards.

WEEK 7:

✓ Take two or three agents from your office to review the property while the sellers are at home. Have a current CMA with you and then have those agents offer suggestions to your sellers.

✓ If agents suggest the sellers stage their house differently or remove furniture, then take new pictures once that is complete.

✓ Rearrange the pictures and rewrite your remarks on MLS.

✓ Re-check MLS listing to make sure it is accurate. If property taxes have changed or HOA dues, update your listing.

✓ Search other websites such as Trulia.com and Realtor.com to verify your listing is still there.

✓ Create a new e-flyer and resend using your e-Marketing with the newly reduced price.

WEEK 8:

✓ Review the remarks on MLS with your seller. Inform them you have rewritten them twice already and encourage them to write remarks too.

✓ If agents have suggested the sellers stage their house differently or remove furniture, then take new pictures once that is complete and replace them on MLS and flyers.

✓ Prepare for another open house, or suggest other agents in your office conduct them.

✓ Replace the flyers in the box on the sign with new clean flyers. Each time the price is changed or you retake pictures, you should update the flyer.

✓ Communicate with your sellers.

✓ Search for an updated list as to how many buyers are registered with saved searches this home fits into. Market your listing to those buyers and agents representing those buyers.

✓ Use MLS to search for every active home nearby. Send

each listing agent the info on your listing. As those agents get calls from potential buyers wanting to see their listing, those buyers might ask those agents what else is for sale. Make sure you remind those listing agents frequently with the details on your house.

WEEK 9:

- ✓ Review all current listings with sellers. Take them to tour other comparable homes nearby. Inform them how long each home has been on the market and if each home has been reduced.
- ✓ Review the price with the sellers.
- ✓ Discuss financing strategies with your loan expert for any additional creative marketing ideas. The listing price has likely changed since their original flyers were printed. Inform your loan expert each time you change the price so they can be printing updated flyers also.

WEEK 10:

- ✓ Communicate with your sellers.
- ✓ Contact other agents with listings nearby to ask how many showings they have. Network with them to gather feedback on activity from showings and their open houses.
- ✓ Organize a Broker/Agent tour of other homes in the neighborhood at the same time to attract more agents.
- ✓ Check the placement of directionals and the For Sale sign from any recent storms that might have caused them to lean.
- ✓ Make sure the flyer box has an adequate number of flyers.
- ✓ Prepare for another open house.

✓ Check how many web views your site is getting and communicate that info to the seller.

✓ Review market activity in this general price range; current number of actives, pending sales, and closings and communicate that info to the seller.

✓ Create a new e-flyer and distribute.

WEEK 11:

✓ Conduct an amazing successful open house as outlined in Chapter 21.

✓ Communicate with your seller everything you did to prepare for the open house. Continue to impress upon your sellers how hard you are working to get their home sold.

✓ Search for an updated list as to how many buyers are registered with saved searches this home fits into. Market your listing to those buyers and agents representing those buyers.

✓ Use MLS to search for every active home nearby. Send each listing agent the info on your new listing. As those agents get calls from potential buyers wanting to see their listing, those buyers might ask those agents what else is for sale. Make sure you remind those listing agents frequently with the details on your house.

WEEK 12:

✓ Review all current listings with seller close to their home. Inform them of all price reductions on the remaining inventory. How many homes have sold? How many new listings have entered the market since theirs came up for sale?

✓ Review the total number of homes for sale in the zip code. How many are under contract and how many have reduced? What is the average number of days on the market?

✓ Offer to show your seller any of these homes so they can compare.

✓ Review a pricing strategy with the seller.

✓ Review staging again.

✓ Review the appearance of the front of the home. Does it need leaves raked or gutters cleaned? Have bushes become overgrown?

✓ If seasons have changed, consider taking a new front picture and update flyers and MLS.

✓ Rewrite the MLS remarks again with your clients.

✓ Review the placement of directionals.

✓ Stay in contact with your seller. Remind your seller it just takes that "one right buyer" and their home is sold. Encourage them to stay positive.

#25 THE SECRET OF SUCCESS IN REACHING YOUR GOALS:

THIS BOOK HAS BEEN FILLED with a variety of suggestions to help make you a success in selling homes, but it all comes down to the one thing every top selling agent has in common. It is the secret to becoming successful. The secret is so powerful it is found evident in nearly every form of great accomplishment.

In the beginning of this book I asked "Why are you doing this?" Why would anyone want to face the risk of rejection on a daily basis? Who would want to take on listings that might never sell? Who would want to deal with nagging sellers constantly bugging you about why they get no showings and what you're doing about it? Why would you want strangers riding around in your car while you show them houses, none of which they might even buy? Each of us must have an internal desire to succeed that is so strong that if you don't succeed, at least you know you died trying. How strong is your desire to succeed? The time is now to help you become more successful than ever.

Let's look at this from a different perspective for a moment. Say a person is overweight by 50 pounds. He has been overweight since high school, but has gained more weight over the past 10 years and is now 29 years old. Is it possible for him to lose the 50 pounds? …or is it impossible? This is a very important question. If such a goal is not even possible then there is no hope in even trying, but if losing weight is achievable then this person needs an action plan to accomplish it. In fact, let's back off from such an overwhelming goal, how about 15 pounds? *Can* he lose 15 pounds? Yes. *Will* he lose 15 pounds?

Sadly, the honest truth is probably not. This person will probably not lose 15 pounds, and for that reason he will probably always be at least 50 pounds overweight and likely get even heavier over the next few years. Why? Because it will take hard work to lose any weight at all, even if this person knows it is possible. It will take a new form of discipline so sacrificing that this person will likely give up before making any significant progress at all. There are bad habits in place that will be extremely hard to break. Our attitudes and desires are the greatest factors motivating us to succeed or they keep us from being all we can be. Sadly, many people settle for mediocrity in some areas of their lives even though they hope for something better. Complacency and a lack of self-discipline are holding many people back. Want proof? Look around everywhere you go. Our nation seems to have more overweight people than ever before. I have no idea why, but many people who have tried to lose weight don't end up reaching their goal. They try but they fall short.

Now let's say this overweight person has a new-found desire to lose weight like never before. He is filled with a passionate desire to accomplish his goal. Let's say *you* want to sell more homes this year. You are sick and tired of just hoping for success. You are ready to do all that it takes to accomplish greatness in your career. What will it take to succeed? What is the secret???

When we set out to accomplish something difficult we need an action plan. An action plan is a detailed to-do list. When you are planning what to cook for the following week you get recipes out and make a list of all the ingredients you need for that entire week. You make a conscious decision to write down what groceries you will need and you make an organized list of what to purchase. You take your list, possibly with the extra work of finding some coupons, and you drive to the grocery store. You have a plan. After investing time at the grocery store (even when you don't really want to go), you go home and organize everything into your pantry getting ready for the upcoming week of cooking. Your organized action plan makes it possible to feed your family with success. We use action plans for nearly everything we accomplish all the time.

Back to the person who wants to lose weight. Can a person who is 50 pounds overweight lose the 50 pounds? Yes he can. How?

Can a person who has experienced a life feeling trapped in jobs working for other people get a real estate license and become the top selling agent in his office a few years later? Yes he can! How?

Let's use a different example now. Take a thin young man who has a strong desire to bulk up and gain some muscle. Can this thin person increase muscle mass within a few months to give a completely different appearance? Yes he can. How?

His action plan is simple. He needs to lift weights about 4 or 5 times a week –every single week for a few months. He needs to eat properly taking in more protein and stay consistent not missing workouts. Sounds easy, but following this action plan daily for a long enough period of time to see success is difficult. His desire is so strong that he buys a workout magazine and starts doing pushups in his room at night. He buys weights and work out equipment and begins performing weight lifting exercises as outlined in the magazine. He has started the process of becoming a success at his goals. The first workouts that beginning week are followed a couple of days later with intense soreness, so he stops for a week to recover. When looking in the mirror, he feels the need to improve again and begins working his action plan the next week instead. He works out 5 times that week and feels like a winner. The next week he also works out 5 times. Now he is on track to succeed but at this point, when he doesn't see any immediate results, he gets discouraged and quits. After looking at the weights on the floor in his room for another month he takes them back to the basement where they collect dust. It's the same in fitness centers all around the country. Every January they are packed with new customers excited about their New Year's resolutions. They gladly pay for a two-year membership and start off strong coming frequently. After a month most of them have quit never to return again because they didn't see results fast enough. In reality, this is what happens many times.

Let's examine a new realtor. This particular agent has been in the business for three months. He currently has no listings, but does have a couple of potential buyers who might buy in the near future. This realtor has no money for mailings and even if he did, his name list is only 20 people. He shows up to the office for board duty, but since he hasn't had a good call in the last 3 weeks, the expectation is there won't be any good calls this week either. He holds an open house every other Sunday for other agents, but hasn't picked up any good buyers yet. This agent is failing. He will not be in the business much longer unless something changes. In reality, this is what happens many times.

All successful people must follow an action plan. It's an organized to-do list of what they should be doing each day. Whether a person has the goal of losing weight, or lifting weights to gain size, or selling homes, they must have clear goals with a check list of what to do consistently to achieve results. Most people also need someone to help motivate them. They need an accountability partner, or a good broker, or a workout partner to help ensure success. Even if they have an accountability partner, they still must have a personal burning desire to succeed or die trying.

DON'T EAT THE ICE CREAM!

We must change our unproductive habits that lead us away from accomplishing our goals. For someone who is losing weight, that person cannot eat ice cream at the end of the evening while watching TV and then go to bed. Those self-defeating decisions are what created this extra weight in the first place. Every person who has accomplished something great in their lives has one thing in common. It is the *secret* of what sets them apart from the others who failed.

THE SECRET: WORK YOUR ACTION PLAN CONSISTENTLY <u>EVERY SINGLE DAY</u>

The secret to becoming a success is to take your to-do list, and accomplish something from it every single day. For an overweight person on track to lose weight he must do something every single day to reach success. For a thin person gaining muscle, he must work out 4 or 5 times a week consistently to achieve success. Daily consistency is the key.

For you as a real estate agent wanting greater success, remember the successful tips in this book. Create a to-do list of what you will do each week and break it down on a daily basis so it all gets done. On Sunday you'll be doing an open house somewhere, and during the previous week you'll be getting prepared. During the week you can work on your name list, prepare a mailing, go door to door, take classes, develop your website, get a new headshot taken, take extra board duty time in your office, go on appointments with agents who will let you listen in, and prospect wherever you are that day at the gym, grocery store, restaurant, etc. At the end of this book are pages for you to write down names to add to your COI list. Write them down as you think of them. Always have your nametag on when out in public. There are SO many things you can be doing each day. Don't waste a valuable day by doing nothing toward your goals. If you want to build muscle you must lift heavy things consistently, and if you want to lose weight you must put down the ice cream. Day after day after day. This is a successful way of living.

It's important to remind yourself why you're a real estate agent. My personal motivation was this. After graduating from college I entered the retail world as a department manager and I really just hated it. I was underpaid and overworked. After a year or so passed, I got a different job in a more corporate environment. I quickly realized I was bored working in my little cubicle and didn't like the corporate structure. I watched people investing years of their lives sitting in similar cubicles trying to rub noses with the right managers in the hopes they would be promoted before fellow co-workers. Too many people hoping for very few promotion opportunities. I dreaded going to work and wanted more control of my future and income. I wanted to help people in a significant way, and I was left unfulfilled in all of my previous jobs. It's important for you to realize what events in your life have brought you into the real estate business. For me, I was sick and tired of dead end jobs and I felt this was the only shot left for me to become a success.

With that desperate attitude I did every single thing I could think of to make it as a realtor. Even when I saw no results happening I continued without fail. Day after day after day, I continued doing what I believed would work even when I saw little or no success at all.

This Is the Crucial Moment Where Most People Make the Biggest Mistakes in Achieving their Goals

An overweight person finally becomes motivated enough to join a fitness center. The desire is strong. He does aerobics twice a week for three weeks. He starts walking on a treadmill at the gym afterwards and starts eating healthier. He is doing exactly what he should to see success, but after three weeks of not seeing results he quits in disgust. What he didn't know was week four would show improvement. Then he might need to continue the same routine for 3 more weeks again not seeing any additional results. But the 8th week would bring a major metabolic change and the weight would quickly begin coming off. Success was coming soon.

Whatever you need to change about yourself will take time to see lasting results, but sadly our society feeds on immediate gratification. We have instant pudding and instant mashed potatoes. It's not true that "a watched pot never boils," because it boils in the same amount of time – we're just too rushed to watch. Our society is thriving on low-maintenance, less effort, and comfortable complacency. Many of these time savers are great. I will be the first to admit that I thoroughly enjoy my self-propelled mower and I love fast food. Many times I rush back home to watch my mega-sized TV getting over 100 channels. And thanks to a DVR we can even eliminate commercials! If I could lay on the couch all day with all my remotes I would be very happy.

Sometimes our society forgets to teach that success requires hard work and discipline, possibly taking a long time to achieve. Delayed gratification doesn't seem to be taught much anymore, yet it is such a vital part of success. If you desire to quit smoking, it will take time for the urges to diminish. If you want to learn to play the piano it will take months of lessons before you really begin playing, and only after consistent practice. No matter what you're working on in your life, you need to do something toward that goal <u>every day</u>. Have you noticed a college class will be spread out over an entire semester meeting 3 times a week for around 16 weeks? It's not all squeezed into one big weekend. If you're going to lose weight you don't fast for 2 days and then eat what you want the rest of the week.

You need a desire so strong that when no one comes to your open house, you don't quit… you prepare for another open house. When you send out a mailing and nobody calls you, you don't quit… you stop by the Post Office and buy more stamps. When you drive a family around for a month showing them houses, and then they buy a FSBO, you don't quit…you pick up another buyer. You work hard to make it, or you die trying. For some of you, if you don't survive as a realtor you have no back-up plan. There might not be another job out there for you in this economy so you really have no other option besides making this work. Can you make this work? YES! You most definitely can make this work.

If you are having a difficult year in real estate, then apply the successful tips from this book and begin again. Put some new-found energy into going the extra mile. In the beginning of this book, you drew a line in front of you. It is now time to step over that line.

With consistent effort you will eventually win the race. Some agents will use all their energy during their first two months in the business and then lose steam becoming frustrated. When running hurdles, you have to pace yourself so you run a consistent race to the finish line. Exhausting everything within you on the first half of the race and then being forced to quit from lack of energy is pointless. It results in failure. But consistently working towards your goals will make you accomplish great things in all areas of your life.

We use water each day. We drink it, bathe with it, water our plants with it, and wash our clothes with it. It has many common daily uses. However when focused consistently over long periods of time, it becomes a powerful force. Beautiful stalactites in a cave are created from water dripping over many years depositing minerals. When consistently applied over a growing season, water can effectively irrigate our nation's farmlands growing crops for millions of people. The Grand Canyon was cut by the slow process of water consistently eroding away the soil. Without having daily consistency over a long enough time, none of these things would be possible.

ACCOMPLISH SOMETHING EVERY SINGLE DAY FROM YOUR ACTION PLAN TO ACHIEVE SUCCESS

A statement, so we're all clear with no misunderstandings: If a person is 50 pounds overweight, and he has a burning desire to do whatever it takes for him to lose that 50 pounds, he will lose it. If a thin young man wants to bulk up and does what it takes with consistent workouts, he will bulk up. If a person has been smoking 2 packs of cigarettes a day for 40 years and she wants to quit badly enough, she will quit. If you create an action plan of what you will do as a realtor, and you work that to-do list every day, you will thrive in this business. Hallelujah! You are becoming the success you always dreamed you could be!

If you want to lose weight, don't eat the ice cream! If you want to sell houses, work your action plan every single day.

I chose to become a realtor and so did you. When I first started my career I was unsure if I would be a success in this business. I drew a line in front of me and vowed I would become a success as a realtor or I would die trying. When my own dad begged me to stop wasting all my money on this business and go get a real job with benefits, I worked harder to show him I could succeed. This business offers more rewards than I could ever imagine – life-long friends, freedom to work from home, flexibility to do anything you want during the day, and the unique opportunity to work as much or as little as you like depending on your goals. Most importantly, it offers unlimited income and the chance to make a real difference in people's lives.

You are in a track meet running hurdles with other agents in a packed stadium. Most agents fail because they only look at the next hurdle coming up, but you place your eyes on the finish line never looking down because you are committed and focused on your goal. As you consistently run the race, you find yourself pulling ahead of the other agents. You set yourself apart as you hear the deafening roar of a cheering crowd watching you achieve greatness in your career. The exhilaration of knowing you are becoming a front runner only adds to your momentum of speed. You are selling homes in a tough market and you are running the race. You can see the finish line coming around the curve. Your friends and family are in the packed stadium watching you race as they give you referrals showing their support along the way. Even though you ache from running and all the consistent hard work, you continue pushing harder even though sometimes you wonder if it's all worth it. You jump over the next few hurdles with even more success! You are listing more houses. You are picking up more buyers, and your income is growing. You are doing what it takes to succeed with consistent effort. You find yourself making a lot of money as a realtor and you are living an amazing lifestyle!

Embrace the hard work it takes to run the race and bask in the wonderful blessings your real estate career will give you. You just cleared the last hurdle heading toward the finish line. All the hard work has been worth it. Overcoming the obstacles and hurdles has been challenging, but the benefits are definitely worth it. You have invested yourself in a life-changing career giving you a foundation of success for years to come. The crowd stands on its feet bearing witness as you cross the line and achieve greatness. There is no doubt that *you* are a successful top selling realtor! The crowd explodes with thunderous applause!

YES! You are selling homes in a tough market. Victory and success are yours!

EXPAND YOUR COI LIST ON THESE PAGES

NAME: _____

ADDRESS: _____

_____

PHONE#: _____

EMAIL: _____

NAME: _____

ADDRESS: _____

_____

PHONE#: _____

EMAIL: _____

NAME: _____

ADDRESS: _____

_____

PHONE#: _____

EMAIL: _____

NAME: _____

ADDRESS: _____

_____

PHONE#: _____

EMAIL: _____

NAME: _____

ADDRESS: _____

_____

PHONE#: _____

EMAIL: _____

EXPAND YOUR COI LIST ON THESE PAGES

NAME: _____

ADDRESS: _____

_____

PHONE#: _____

EMAIL: _____

NAME: _____

ADDRESS: _____

_____

PHONE#: _____

EMAIL: _____

NAME: _____

ADDRESS: _____

_____

PHONE#: _____

EMAIL: _____

NAME: _____

ADDRESS: _____

_____

PHONE#: _____

EMAIL: _____

NAME: _____

ADDRESS: _____

_____

PHONE#: _____

EMAIL: _____

EXPAND YOUR COI LIST ON THESE PAGES

NAME: _____

ADDRESS: _____

_____

PHONE#: _____

EMAIL: _____

NAME: _____

ADDRESS: _____

_____

PHONE#: _____

EMAIL: _____

NAME: _____

ADDRESS: _____

_____

PHONE#: _____

EMAIL: _____

NAME: _____

ADDRESS: _____

_____

PHONE#: _____

EMAIL: _____

NAME: _____

ADDRESS: _____

_____

PHONE#: _____

EMAIL: _____

EXPAND YOUR COI LIST ON THESE PAGES

NAME: _____
ADDRESS: _____
_____
PHONE#: _____
EMAIL: _____

NAME: _____
ADDRESS: _____
_____
PHONE#: _____
EMAIL: _____

NAME: _____
ADDRESS: _____
_____
PHONE#: _____
EMAIL: _____

NAME: _____
ADDRESS: _____
_____
PHONE#: _____
EMAIL: _____

NAME: _____
ADDRESS: _____
_____
PHONE#: _____
EMAIL: _____

EXPAND YOUR COI LIST ON THESE PAGES

NAME: _____

ADDRESS: _____

_____

PHONE#: _____

EMAIL: _____

NAME: _____

ADDRESS: _____

_____

PHONE#: _____

EMAIL: _____

NAME: _____

ADDRESS: _____

_____

PHONE#: _____

EMAIL: _____

NAME: _____

ADDRESS: _____

_____

PHONE#: _____

EMAIL: _____

NAME: _____

ADDRESS: _____

_____

PHONE#: _____

EMAIL: _____

EXPAND YOUR COI LIST ON THESE PAGES

NAME: _____

ADDRESS: _____

_____

PHONE#: _____

EMAIL: _____

NAME: _____

ADDRESS: _____

_____

PHONE#: _____

EMAIL: _____

NAME: _____

ADDRESS: _____

_____

PHONE#: _____

EMAIL: _____

NAME: _____

ADDRESS: _____

_____

PHONE#: _____

EMAIL: _____

NAME: _____

ADDRESS: _____

_____

PHONE#: _____

EMAIL: _____

EXPAND YOUR COI LIST ON THESE PAGES

NAME: _____

ADDRESS: _____

_____

PHONE#: _____

EMAIL: _____

NAME: _____

ADDRESS: _____

_____

PHONE#: _____

EMAIL: _____

NAME: _____

ADDRESS: _____

_____

PHONE#: _____

EMAIL: _____

NAME: _____

ADDRESS: _____

_____

PHONE#: _____

EMAIL: _____

NAME: _____

ADDRESS: _____

_____

PHONE#: _____

EMAIL: _____

EXPAND YOUR COI LIST ON THESE PAGES

NAME: _____

ADDRESS: _____

_____

PHONE#: _____

EMAIL: _____

NAME: _____

ADDRESS: _____

_____

PHONE#: _____

EMAIL: _____

NAME: _____

ADDRESS: _____

_____

PHONE#: _____

EMAIL: _____

NAME: _____

ADDRESS: _____

_____

PHONE#: _____

EMAIL: _____

NAME: _____

ADDRESS: _____

_____

PHONE#: _____

EMAIL: _____

CPSIA information can be obtained at www.ICGtesting.com
Printed in the USA
LVOW062027131011

250422LV00003B/2/P